Praise for Mother

"A brave, sensitive, and clinically ...tuitive book
filled with wisdom and healing."

— **Erica Komisar, LCSW**, psychoanalyst, parent guidance
expert and author of *Being There: Why Prioritizing
Motherhood in the First Three Years Matters*

"I read *Mother Hunger* as if it was a sacred text—
each word revealing and illuminating the deepest inner
essence of me I knew was there but couldn't name.
Kelly McDaniel has translated the most palpable, potent,
and impactful imprint of mother to daughter that has the power
to heal us in real time while also providing healing to those
who've come before us and arrive after. I honestly cannot
remember a time I have resonated with anything as much as
I do *Mother Hunger*. If you're drawn to this book — trust it!"

— **Nancy Levin**, author of *Setting Boundaries Will Set You Free*

"*Mother Hunger* is a deeply compassionate, scholarly, and
thoughtful journey of understanding into the tender wounds of
our unmet needs. With graceful clarity, Kelly McDaniel guides
the reader through awareness of the impact that nurturing,
protection, and guidance play in our development and creates
compassion for the substitutes we seek when those needs are
not met. Kelly skillfully outlines steps to healing and invites the
reader into growth and hope. This book is a powerful resource!"

— **Jenna Riemersma, LPC**, best-selling author of
*Altogether You: Experiencing personal and spiritual
transformation with Internal Family Systems therapy* and founder
and clinical director of The Atlanta Center for Relational Healing

"With over thirty years of feminist study under
her belt, coupled with decades of treating women
with attachment wounds, McDaniel is uniquely qualified
to write this book. Comprehensive, clear, and
deeply compassionate, *Mother Hunger* is a love letter
to women looking to find their way home."

— **Alexandra Katehakis, Ph.D.**, author of *Sex Addiction as Affect
Dysregulation: A Neurobiologically Informed Holistic Treatment*

"Women often feel broken or irreparably wounded when they don't find the safety, bonding, or unconditional love they need from their mothers. Kelly McDaniel is an expert at explaining how these unmet needs result in women experiencing 'Mother Hunger.' She explains the typical trauma re-enactment that produces low self-esteem, addiction including love and sex, and the ongoing wounding that occurs because of this primary attachment issue. *Mother Hunger* is the road map that will help you repair your sense of self and learn how to heal the most basic need to feel love for oneself. Kelly takes you through the step-by-step process of what you need to do to give yourself the love you didn't know that you deserved"

— **Carol Juergensen Sheets, LCSW, CSAT, CCPS-C**, co-author of *Transformations: A Women's Journey of Self Discovery, Help Her Heal: An Empathy Workbook for Sex Addicts to Help their Partners Heal*, and *Unleashing Your Power: Moving Through the Trauma of Partner Betrayal*

"Kelly McDaniel's *Mother Hunger* is going to create a worldwide sigh of relief as daughters everywhere finally have words to describe the aching loss that haunts their lives and relationships. With compassionate understanding for the incredible challenges that all mothers face when trying to mother well, *Mother Hunger* provides a much-needed key to the hidden impacts that being under-mothered can create and points the way toward healing and wholeness."

— **Michelle Mays LPC, CSAT-S**, founder of PartnerHope and the Center for Relational Recovery

"This book is a must-read. Kelly McDaniel skillfully guides the reader through the delicate and often precarious terrain of attachment trauma. Without any hint of parental blame or shame, McDaniel compassionately provides much-needed information for this often overlooked topic."

— **Britt Frank**, MSW, LSCSW, SEP, licensed psychotherapist and trauma specialist

MOTHER HUNGER

ALSO BY
KELLY MCDANIEL

READY TO HEAL:
Breaking Free of Addictive Relationships

MOTHER HUNGER

How Adult Daughters Can
Understand and Heal from
Lost Nurturance, Protection,
and Guidance

KELLY McDANIEL

HAY HOUSE, INC.
Carlsbad, California • New York City
London • Sydney • New Delhi

Copyright © 2021 by Kelly McDaniel

Published in the United States by: Hay House, Inc.: www.hayhouse
.com® • *Published in Australia by:* Hay House Australia Pty. Ltd.: www.
hayhouse.com.au • *Published in the United Kingdom by:* Hay House UK,
Ltd.: www.hayhouse.co.uk • *Published in India by:* Hay House Publishers
India: www.hayhouse.co.in

Cover design: Kathleen Lynch
Interior design: Julie Davison

Cataloging-in-Publication Data is on file at the Library of Congress

Tradepaper ISBN: 978-1-4019-6085-8
E-book ISBN: 978-1-4019-6086-5
Audiobook ISBN: 978-1-4019-6662-1

17 16 15 14 13 12 11 10 9 8
1st edition, July 2021

Printed in the United States of America

CONTENTS

FOREWORD

My mother died when I was 18 years old, while I was a freshman at a small liberal arts college in Vermont. Ten years later, I wrote her a letter, as I did every year on the anniversary of her death. "Dear Mom," I wrote. "You have been dead for ten years." I am already crying, tears streaming down my cheeks, warm and lucid.

"This letter will be different from the others," I wrote. "Things aren't the same anymore. It has taken these 10 years for me to finally start to care about myself. I never realized how much I hated myself. How afraid of myself I was. This last year has been terribly hard and wonderfully healing. I'm alone now. All alone. No more alcohol, no more boys, no more self-destruction, no more hiding from all the pain. Just me, here and alone. And I still miss you so much. Ten years feels like a lifetime. I am no longer the girl I once was . . . the girl who had a mother.

"But I don't want to do this anymore. Obsess over your death. I don't want my whole life to be about you. I am grateful, so incredibly grateful, for who I have become because of this loss, but I don't want my life to revolve around it anymore.

"And I don't want to be terrible to myself anymore. I don't want to hide. I don't want to feel desperate or lonely or hateful anymore. I want to stride forward. I want to shirk the heavy weight of all this loss. I want to throw it off like a coat worn on a summer day. I am tired of it all. I want to just be me. And to do that, I have to let you go.

"And I think that maybe, just maybe, in letting you go, in not trying to hold on to you, I can be at peace. I haven't been at peace, Mom. All these last 10 years, I've been in so much pain. It's been so hard. And I don't want to do it anymore. But Mom, I need you to release me as well.

"Love, your only daughter, Claire."

This letter is difficult for me to reread now, almost 25 years after her death. My heart breaks for the younger version of me who wrote this letter. And my heart breaks for my mother, who never would have wanted me to feel so much pain.

Three years after I wrote that letter, I gave birth to my first child, a daughter. And in those early weeks and months after she was born, I sat in the nursery holding her in my arms, and I wept. My mother-in-law worried that I had postpartum. She remarked that she didn't remember ever having cried so much when her children were born.

But it wasn't postpartum. It was the realization that I had not let my mother go, that I never would. And that I didn't have to. Holding my daughter in my arms, I knew that the reason I missed my mother so much was because of the same thing I was experiencing right there in the nursery with my own infant: that primal mother-daughter relationship. I realized that this is a love and a bond that runs so deep that no woman could ever deny the presence, or lack, of it.

I've now been a therapist specializing in grief for over a decade. I've sat with hundreds, maybe thousands, of women as they have processed their own mother loss. The profound depth of emotion that comes with the absence of a mother never ceases to amaze me. Whether a woman loses her mother to death, as I did, or to abandonment in its many forms, the experience will be one that a woman will reckon with for her entire life.

When Kelly McDaniel first told me the title of her book *Mother Hunger*, I knew in an instant that this would be a book that would change the lives of everyone who read it. While there have been many books written about loss, and some about mother loss in particular, none have ever so succinctly addressed the experience of what it means to long for a mother.

I see many versions of mother loss in my work as a therapist. I see women who have lost their mothers recently and women who have lost mothers decades ago. I see women who lost their mothers to cancer, suicide, murder, accidents, and illness. And I see women who still have their mothers but have lost them to abandonment, addiction, memory malfunction, mental illness, and more. Some of the losses are more traumatic than others but the experience of longing that comes with this loss is the same. The Mother Hunger these women carry shapes each of them in unique and lasting ways—all of which Kelly addresses in this profoundly brave book.

But in my eyes, what Kelly does most importantly in *Mother Hunger* is validate the experience of mother loss. The phrase I hear from my clients more than any other is *I can't believe I'm still dealing with this.* But as Kelly illustrates, the experience of yearning for a mother affects women on such deep levels that it is often carried not just throughout a woman's lifetime but even passed down through generations.

That *Mother Hunger* not only validates this impact but provides us with solutions and pathways to heal from it, will have ripple effects for years to come.

It took me a long time to forgive myself for being so affected by my mother's death, but for many women, escaping the pain of mother loss is elusive and hard-won. Kelly's book will change that forever. Knowing that *Mother Hunger* is now out in the world, waiting to be found by the women who need it most, eases my heart and gives me hope that healing is possible.

If I were to write my mother another letter today, I would tell her that I didn't let her go all those years ago, that I'll never stop loving her, and yet I've found ways to be at peace in my life. I hope the same becomes true for all who read this book.

Claire Bidwell Smith, LCPC
author of *Anxiety: The Missing Stage of Grief*

INTRODUCTION

In her beautifully written memoir, *Our Lady of Perpetual Hunger*, Lisa Donovan writes:

> We carry one another's pain so deeply, the women in my family. It is like an extra organ, a broken chamber of our hearts that none of us knows how to make work, blocking the normal things that other people's hearts do.[1]

Donovan captures the heartbreak, the "broken chamber," that some daughters inherit from their mothers. While I was writing the book you now hold in your hands, Donovan's words were medicine for my soul, an acknowledgment of the legacy of ancestral heartbreak. It is a topic that is hard to speak about, write about, or know about.

Over the course of two years, I almost stopped writing this manuscript—partly because I'm frequently reminded how much most folks don't want to know about this issue, but mostly because it's just plain hard. Routinely, I asked myself, *Why do this?* I kept going for one reason: this is the book I wish I had as a young woman.

Born to a dynamic line of women who raised children the best they could, I come from a painful background like many of you. Although I benefit from white skin, a robust education, and other advantages, even a life of privilege can't protect someone from Mother Hunger.

My maternal great-grandmother abandoned my grandmother when she was a small girl. She took her other daughter and left town to live with a new man, ultimately one of five men she would marry and divorce. The little girl she left behind grew up to become my grandmother.

I loved my grandmother desperately. We only visited once a year, but those shared times were magical for me. My mother didn't like my grandmother very much. Undoubtedly, the legacy of abandonment had left my grandmother hungry for something my mother had no business providing. It must have been a burden to be her daughter. I don't know the specifics, because my mother has very little memory of her childhood and isn't inclined to talk about these things.

I didn't fully comprehend the concept of Mother Hunger until well into my own motherhood journey and career path. But even at a young age, I knew something was wrong in my family. With hindsight and clinical perspective, I don't think having more information could have helped me while in my mother's care; I was too busy trying to be a good daughter. I was busy surviving. Fortunately, early in my 20s, I stumbled into women's studies courses where I found relevant, eye-opening guidance that gave me ingredients for naming Mother Hunger. Fast forward 20 years to the publication of my first book, *Ready to Heal*, where I first named Mother Hunger as the root of addictive love. Since then, I've been helping women understand and heal the heartache that emerges from poor early attachment. *Mother Hunger: How Adult Daughters Can Understand and Heal from Lost Nurturance, Protection, and Guidance* is a collection of wisdom gleaned from the past three decades of research, practice, and learning. It's a letter from me to you—from one daughter to another—about the legacy of living with a heartbreak that is part biological, part psychological, part cultural, and part spiritual.

In spite of diverse stories, what I've found is that each woman with Mother Hunger yearns for the same thing: a certain quality of love—a nurturing, safe, inspiring love—the kind of love we think of as maternal love. It is the love that we need for a firm start in life. It is an *unconditional* love that no romantic relationship, friendship, or birthday cake can replace.

Many feel this singular love can also be offered by fathers. While it's clear that daughters raised by attentive, nurturing fathers have many advantages, fathers can't replace mothers. Naming Mother Hunger isn't about dismissing the importance of fathers or other primary caregivers. Nor is it about blaming mothers for what they couldn't provide. Mother Hunger is a framework to help you identify what the essential elements of maternal care are so you can recognize what you lost and reclaim what you need.

In this book, we will explore what causes Mother Hunger and what to do about it. As you read these pages and make discoveries, the healing power of recognition won't always feel good, but it will bring you fresh hope and renewed energy. Rest assured that Mother Hunger can be healed without your mother's physical presence or recognition of your sorrow. Mother Hunger doesn't mean you want to be a mother or need to be close to your mother. Mother Hunger can happen whether you were raised by your own mother, an adoptive mother, a foster mother, a father, two mothers, two fathers, a single mother, or multiple caregivers. Mother Hunger is less about who actually raised you than it is about which developmental needs were missing during your formative years. Mother Hunger names the longing that you live with; the yearning for a certain quality of love.

The following chapters are organized to gently support you. In the first chapter, we define Mother Hunger so that right away you find relief. The rest of the book will detail the three essential elements of maternal love. Starting with the maternal element of nurturance, we will learn from animals, talk about attachment, and take a closer look at the complicated relationship with food and sex that is part of Mother Hunger.

From there, we will move on to the second essential maternal element of protection. A review of the turbulent cultural forces that damage women will build compassion for why so many of us have symptoms of Mother Hunger. The true-life case of "Dirty John" illustrates the tragedy that happens when a mother can't protect her daughter and shows how fear is woven into the fabric of being female.

Next, we will explore the third essential maternal element of guidance: how a mother inspires her daughter. Then, as we near the end of the book, we will take a look at Third-Degree Mother Hunger, a relational third-degree burn that can devastate a woman's life, as it did with both Judy Garland and Édith Piaf. Lastly, we will examine the grief embedded in Mother Hunger.

Mother Hunger comes in different forms, some more severe than others, so healing looks different for everyone. Some of you no longer have a living mother, so your path will be different from those who do. Whether your mother is alive or not, healing involves replacing what was lost during your formative years. Not all the ideas in this book will fit your experience as a daughter. But somewhere in these chapters, you may find the right words for the pain that haunts you. When you do, fresh clarity directs your innate healing process.

While your recovery path is unique, there are some common signs of healing that you can look forward to: increased emotional security, an easier time making decisions, less anxiety, and an understanding of your attachment style. You will find compassion for the choices you have made (even the ones you most regret), and it will become easier to select friends and partners who are kind and respectful. If you have children, loving them becomes easier too.

Mother Hunger is not uncommon. But without a name, it hides in secrecy and shame. Giving yourself permission to learn and talk about this relational injury is radical. It is a brave step toward reclaiming the love you need.

If you *are* a mother, it might be tempting to read this book as mothering instructions or to revisit things you regret. Try not to do this. *Please read this book as a daughter.* This book is about learning what you missed during your development so that you can reclaim the tender parts of yourself that were sacrificed to earn your mother's love or survive her absence. As you piece together the story of being your mother's daughter, you will find new resources for lost nurturance, protection, and guidance. Facing the heartbreak that's running your life opens opportunities for joy and connection.

In the pages ahead, as you gather new awareness, my wholehearted support is with you.

CHAPTER 1

NAMING
MOTHER HUNGER

If there were a job description for motherhood, it might look something like this:

> Ideal candidate must be a self-starter, able to comfort and bond with a new, vulnerable human by holding, feeding, and responding to nonverbal cues. Responsibilities include protecting this human from external threats and actively engaging in their academic, spiritual, and social development. Candidate needs equal parts tenderness and strength, grace under pressure, and healthy boundaries. This job is unpaid.

Why would anyone sign up for this job? It's demanding, often thankless, and the pay is terrible. A mother's work is astounding. Isolation, financial stress, and gender discrimination compound the overwhelming responsibilities that come with nurturing and protecting a newborn and guiding a child through complex stages of human development. Additionally, mothering and motherhood is overly romanticized (or dramatized), making it taboo to describe the reality as anything short of a divine experience (or a horrendous burden); both extremes erase the complexity of mothering. When a woman feels "less than" for choosing mothering over other types of work or is judged for placing her career aspirations on hold, something is very wrong with our collective thinking.

Maternal love is our first experience of what love feels like, and the maternal care we receive informs how we feel about ourselves throughout life. Mothering is the most important human endeavor there is. And yet when we try to define what makes a good mother, it's difficult to find the right words. We are without an accurate, universal definition for *mother* or *mothering*.

When I look up *mothering*, the Cambridge Dictionary defines it as "the process of caring for children as their mother or of caring for people in the way a mother does." Merriam-Webster defines *mothering* as "to bring forth from the womb; to give birth to." These definitions give us nothing concrete; they imply mothering is simple and innate to females.

To help women heal Mother Hunger, I needed a working definition of mothering. It's taken me years of listening to brokenhearted adult women and a thorough exploration of attachment theory to create a framework that can guide the treatment process. What I've found is that mothering requires three essential elements: nurturance, protection, and guidance. The first two—nurturance and protection—are the most primitive needs little ones have from mothers. Guidance, the third element, comes later. If we are deprived of one or more of these developmental needs, we struggle with symptoms of insecure attachment as we mature. For example, without early maternal nurturance, we grow up hungry for touch and belonging. Without early maternal protection, we are constantly anxious and afraid. Without maternal guidance, we lack an internal compass directing our choices. These are the symptoms of Mother Hunger.

Mother Hunger may sound like another excuse to blame mothers for our problems, but it's not. In fact, it's quite the opposite. When we understand that mothers love us the best way they can and the only way they know how, blame has no place. A mother can only give her child what she has.

Mother Hunger emerges from the intergenerational inheritance of growing up in a culture that prefers men, masculine traits, and independence while devaluing women, feminine traits, and interdependence. If we can put aside mother blaming, or the tendency to make sweeping generalizations about women juggling careers and thus struggling to be present to their families, our collective understanding of Mother Hunger could guide an inspired effort to support women in preparation for motherhood. After all, in the long run, everyone benefits from nurturing, protective, maternal care and guidance.

We Need Our Mothers

If you have ever felt too needy or dependent, this section might help you understand why. We need our mothers. This need is biologically hardwired into our bodies and brains. If we didn't have enough mothering, yearning for love stays with us. By *mother*, I'm primarily referencing the biological mother—but *mother* is also a verb, and an adult with the desire, ability, and willingness to nurture, protect, and guide a child can be a mother. However, I appreciate and agree with Erica Komisar's observation in *Being There*: "Our denial of the very specific and special physical and emotional role of a mother to her child, particularly in our attempts to be modern, is not in the best interest of children and their needs."[1] Like Komisar, I have a front-row seat in my practice to what happens when this important relationship is compromised.

Mothering is a consuming occupation because little ones come with powerful survival instincts. From the very beginning of life, instincts compel newborns to stay close to their biological mother, as her voice, smell, and body are already familiar. She is *home*. Like adults who want one primary lover or a best friend, babies thrive in a familiar, soothing relationship during the early months. This is biology.

When the biological mother can't be available, an individual other than the biological mother can be the primary caregiver. Sometimes, however, as in the case of medical emergency, maternal death, or adoption, an initial separation from the biological mother's body can add complications for bonding with an alternate caregiver. According to adoption expert Dr. Marcy Axness, "Nature is a strict taskmaster: neither the best intentions nor the noblest justifications can rewrite her laws of neurophysiology."[2] Axness researches and writes primarily about adoption and adoptees, working to solve the "social science riddle" that explains why adoptees have more mental health problems than non-adoptees. She cites Dr. Gabor Maté, who says that adults who were adopted as infants "harbor a powerful and lifelong sense of rejection."[3] The work of Maté and Axness teaches us a great deal about our earliest life processes and how risky separation from our mother can be. I love Axness's insights here:

> Tremendous blessings can be experienced by all the participants in adoption, but we must never

forget that most often, those blessings are born from loss—the loss for the birthparents of a child they will not parent; the loss of their dreamed-of biological child the adoptive parents won't have; and the loss for the adopted child of his or her biological, genealogical, and possibly cultural connections. . . . Compassionate care for the separation trauma, loss, and grief suffered by a newborn under any circumstances—adoption, surrogacy, NICU care—needn't wait a moment; it can and should begin immediately.[4]

A baby who has experienced an abrupt loss of her biological mother requires extra care and recognition of separation distress. When this doesn't happen, the early rupture can cause lifelong heartache. If this is part of your story, I hope it's validating to know that early maternal separation is a hardship.

Missing Maternal Care

Mother Hunger is a term I created to describe what it feels like to grow up without a quality of mothering that imprints emotional worth and relational security. Mother Hunger feels like an emptiness in the soul that is hard to describe because it may set in during infancy or before language forms and become part of how you always feel. The term *Mother Hunger* captures a compelling, insatiable yearning for love—the sort of love we dream about but can't find. Many of us mistake Mother Hunger for a craving for romantic love. But in truth, we are longing for the love we didn't receive during our formative moments, months, and years.

Essential elements of maternal care provide the environment for a robust, healthy brain that is ready for bonding and learning. Babies need reliable, sensitive human closeness in order for the brain to develop the necessary social areas for human connection. Our first love, a mother's love, teaches us how love will feel in the future. "Today, when fathers are more involved in raising their children than ever before, the idea of the unique and irreplaceable role of a mother may seem old-fashioned. And yet there is significant evidence that biology has an impact on the different ways men and women nurture, and the most recent research has shown that a mother's unique presence is critical to the emotional development and mental health of her children in their early years."[5]

Hungry to Attach

If you are reading this book, it's likely that sometimes you feel crazy, ashamed, or broken—but you aren't. Mother Hunger is deeply misunderstood, and people who don't have Mother Hunger simply can't relate to what it feels like. This, of course, leaves us feeling alone with all our confusing emotions and behaviors.

In 2008, I used prevailing clinical language to describe Mother Hunger as an *attachment disorder*. I regret this terminology, because Mother Hunger isn't a disorder, it's an *injury*—a heartbreak that forms from inadequate maternal nurturance, protection, or guidance in early development. *Injury* aptly describes Mother Hunger, because living with it hurts—all the time. It's like grief—complicated grief that comes from carrying an unacknowledged, invisible burden all by yourself.

As a child, if essential elements of maternal nurturance and protection were missing, you didn't stop loving your mother—you simply didn't learn to love yourself. This is the essence of Mother Hunger. Mother Hunger is a heartbreak that touches everything in your world, particularly your relationships with others and your own sense of worth. In this book, I will explain this concept from many perspectives—biological, emotional, and psychological—so that you no longer feel confused, crazy, or alone.

In attachment theory language, Mother Hunger is a way to rename *insecure attachment*. Insecure attachment is a bothersome label, because it implies that something is wrong with you and how you relate to others. No one wants to be called insecure. But insecure attachment is not a character weakness. It's a term, created for research purposes, that categorizes how you attach to others, which is a direct result of how you were nurtured and protected as a child. At least 50 percent of the population has an insecure attachment style (we look at this more closely in the next chapter), so if your early years left you with an undesirable or untrustworthy experience of relationships, you're in good company.[6]

When early needs for nurturance and protection aren't met, it's a setup for Mother Hunger to grow. Although many adults have Mother Hunger, it shows up differently for each of us. Based on which maternal element was missing, for how long, and to what degree, your hunger may be mild or severe.

Mother Hunger comes from events that may happen before language is formed, when a mother's care is your entire world. To get an idea of this, think of your biological mother as your first home. Her body, embrace, and emotions were your first environment, inseparable from your newborn body and emotions. For an infant, a mother's body is the natural habitat that regulates breathing, body temperature, sleep rhythms, and heart rate. Nature's design is for her to stay close so that your development goes smoothly.

When a baby is alerted to a need by hunger, pain, or separation, nature's design is for her mother's soothing touch and sounds to meet that need. Over time, with maternal responsiveness, positive interactions strengthen the developmental reward systems that help us trust others and manage stress. In this way, the daily interactions and nighttime comfort between mother and child "are the neurobiological glue for all future healthy relationships."[7]

If for whatever reason your mother was not ready to be a mother, or if, like many, she was unaware of the concepts we will cover here, science suggests that you may carry the ambivalence, fear, or anger that she felt. Her responsiveness to your needs and her physical presence may have been inadequate. Although you have no clear memory of her early care, your body does. When essential elements of maternal care were absent, the result is an attachment injury that becomes the foundation of future thinking and feeling.

Implicit Memory

Your body knows the story of how early love felt. For this reason, much of the focus of this book will be on the first two years of life, before memory is explicit and cognition is available, when "thinking" isn't thinking at all—it's feeling. Infant and toddler "thought" is a body-based, emotional experience informed by the early environment.[8]

Since the thinking brain, or neocortex, develops sometime after age three (when children start asking "Why?" a lot), logic isn't available before then.[9] We can think of it like this: For a baby, feelings are facts. If baby is afraid or hungry and a sensitive adult responds to her cues, all is well. If no one is there, all is not well. Separation from a familiar caregiver means danger.

Emotions are stored in the body and create a certain reality or belief system: *The world is safe and so am I* or *The world is scary and I'm all alone.* Stored sensations like these become implicit memories. Unlike explicit memory that is conscious and has language, implicit memory is unconscious and has none. Implicit memories reside deep within the limbic structures of the brain, silently whispering messages of safety or danger to the rest of the body. Early experiences impact the developing central nervous system through feelings and bodily sensations. In this way, "remembering" things from your early years is more of a sensation than a conscious awareness.

Feelings create implicit memory from preverbal, precognitive moments with and without our mother. Early emotional experiences literally become embedded in the architecture of our brain.[10] When an infant's vulnerable nervous system picks up that things are not safe, as with early maternal separations or insensitive care, nature calls forth a fear response. Fear releases cortisol and adrenaline, which can be toxic for developing brain regions. When fear isn't soothed and happens regularly, a baby stores the fearful sensations in her cells, building a body and brain poised for danger—hungry for love but wary of human connection.

Understanding implicit memory explains why sometimes we have no idea why we act the way we do. We can't see the distress living in our body. Early memories are dissociated from consciousness, but they direct our moods and our health throughout life.[11] Dr. Daniel J. Siegel talks about the importance of integrating implicit and explicit memory so that you gain insight into how your past is impacting you. You are doing that now by acknowledging Mother Hunger and learning how to heal it.

Human Connection

The first environment each and every one of us experiences is our biological mother. In utero, her emotions and nutrition inform us about the world we are entering and how to live in it. Our sense of belonging begins here. Human connection—our ability to bond with and trust others—is first developed in the womb and continues growing within a suitable primary relationship so that we are ready for social bonds with others.

We know that the largest predictor of human health and happiness isn't wealth or status; it's the number of loving relationships we have. The basis of lifelong psychobiological well-being is established during the first 1,000 days of our lives. Dr. Allan Schore, world leader in attachment theory, stresses the importance of the first 1,000 days, which encompass conception to age two. He calls these first days "the origin of the early forming subjective implicit self."[12]

Neuroscience informs us that the brain doesn't differentiate emotional pain from physical pain. The body can't tell the difference between a broken bone and a broken heart. An infant who is hungry or lonely feels pain. When there isn't a close caregiver to relieve her, the pain intensifies. Her brain can't inform her body about *why* she's in pain. If maternal care is compromised during the first three years, this lack of nurturance is heartbreaking for a baby.

The science is irrefutable: children need nurturance, protection, and guidance from their early caregivers in order to develop the necessary brain processes for optimal living. The Centers for Disease Control and Prevention (CDC) identifies "safe, stable, and nurturing relationships" (SSNRs) as foundational for promoting the healthy social and emotional development of children. Within the context of SSNRs, adults can buffer children's fight-or-flight responses in the face of stressors. These relationships further allow children to optimize positive personal development and promote their social skills. The CDC defines *safe*, *stable*, and *nurturing* as follows:

- **Safety:** The extent to which a child is free from fear and secure from physical or psychological harm within their social and physical environments.

- **Stability:** The degree of predictability and consistency in a child's social, emotional, and physical environment.

- **Nurturing:** The extent to which children's physical, emotional, and developmental needs are sensitively and consistently met.[13]

Note: While advocating for children, the CDC also emphasizes that adults need SSNRs with other adults, often referred to as *social support* or *social capital*, to maintain nurturing relationships with their children. The Center for Health Care Strategies explains how "one critical outcome of SSNR is secure attachment."[14]

We can't expect infants and children not to have these needs simply because they are inconvenient for us to meet. The cost of ignoring them is too great. As Erica Komisar points out, "We want to eradicate mental health issues like depression, anxiety, and violence in children and young adults, but we don't really want to look too deeply at the root of the problem."[15] If we look too closely, major changes would be required of us to remedy systemic issues of parental leave and misogynistic life forces that objectify and disempower women. We will take a closer look at patriarchy in Chapter 6: Protection.

Belonging Is Survival

Birth isn't supposed to feel like leaving home. Babies are designed to stay physically close to their biological mothers, their most familiar environment. Mothers are shelter and nourishment. In the first six to nine months of life, babies can't distinguish the self from the mother.[16] This is nature's plan to ensure infant survival. Baby brains and bodies are built for close care with the mother, which means being carried, held, and nursed. Babies simply aren't designed for long hours away from their primary caregiver; immature developing systems like breathing, heart rate, temperature, and emotional security rely on human touch and proximity.

I want my mommy is the universally recognized plea of a distressed toddler. We've heard this cry. Maybe we've felt this cry; the plea echoes deeply inside our hearts. What happens when cries go unanswered? Or meet irritated, impatient responses? Do we stop needing our mom? Not at all. Over time, without maternal comfort, we do learn to bury the need. But the need doesn't go away. Unmet needs for maternal nurturance and protection fester like an angry infection. The body holds the memory of emotional pain and, over time, may generate chronic distress and insecurity. When distress is the norm, it becomes toxic. Toxic stress creates physiological inflammation, weakening the immune system. In this way, lack of early nurturance or protection is a form of adversity and creates an attachment injury. The frightened or lonely toddler within follows us into adulthood, wreaking havoc on our bodies, relationships, and careers.[17] This early broken heart is the root of Mother Hunger.

"No One Loves You Like Your Mother"

The truth is, we never really outgrow our need for a mother to comfort us, celebrate our accomplishments, or make us soup. To quote author Adrienne Rich, "There was, is, in most of us, a girl-child still longing for a woman's nurturance, tenderness, and approval."[18] For daughters, healthy maternal love always feels good. Mothers and daughters who remain in warm connection throughout their life span are both healthier and happier than those who are lost to each other.

Mothers who provide adequate nurturance, protection, and guidance create securely attached daughters who navigate life's challenges without unnecessary distress. But the myth that all mothers love their daughters erases the truth that many women know: maternal love didn't feel good. The fantasy of maternal love did not apply The myth creates confusion for many daughters who never knew this kind of tenderness.

Mother Hunger—yearning for maternal love—can come from well-meaning mothers who could not be there or from mothers who *were* there and *wanted* to love but did not have the proper infrastructure for attachment programmed into their own psyches. Mother Hunger does not discriminate based on race or class, because infant needs are universal. The kind of care we received as infants and toddlers teaches us whether we are worthy, lovable, and safe. Truly, what I've found is that having an unkind or neglectful mother can be as damaging as having no mother at all.

Daughters of compromised mothers cling to hope— hope that the mother they have will become the mother they *need*. Enduring hope creates a pathological fantasy that keeps women trapped in cycles of disappointment and grief. Choices feel more like compulsions. Decision-making is based on external pressures rather than internal values. Substitutes are needed. In childhood, surrogate mothers may look a lot like cake, ice cream, or fairy tales. But eventually, vodka, drugs, or hasty, head-over-heels relationships take their place. In all stages of life, untreated Mother Hunger craves a quick fix for the empty hole lurking inside.

"Motherless" Daughters

After publishing my first book, *Ready to Heal*, women who identified with Mother Hunger sought my support. I needed better language to describe the wordless despair that followed adult daughters into boardrooms, restaurants, romance, and motherhood. Hope Edelman's book *Motherless Daughters* magically came across my path. Edelman, a gifted journalist and writer, lost her own mother prematurely. She found language for the emotional legacy of being a motherless daughter, expertly describing the emotional, social, and psychological arrested development that happens without maternal care. Her book fascinated me because her descriptions of motherless daughters sounded like my clients, even though most of my clients still had living mothers.

To make sense of this, I found the important work of Dr. Pauline Boss on ambiguous loss. *Ambiguous loss* is a term she coined to explain what happens when someone we love changes, as in the case of dementia, Alzheimer's disease, or a traumatic brain injury. It occurs when psychological absence co-exists with physical presence—in other words, when a person is physically present but psychologically and emotionally absent. Boss's description helped me understand why my clients looked like Edelman's motherless daughters.

A daughter may grow up with motherless symptoms because she is missing her mother's attention and attunement. Attention is essential to nurturing and protecting. To feel loved, children need their mother's emotional attunement as well as her physical presence. The absence of maternal emotional availability directly impacts the quality of her care. Lack of maternal attunement happens for many reasons, such as work demands, smartphones and screens, various addictions, or poor health. A mother's own unhealed psychological coping can impair her capacity for attention and attunement, removing her from the present moment and her daughter.

A Mother Is First a Daughter

When I need language for Mother Hunger, Adrienne Rich always inspires me. Rich writes:

> Many of us were mothered in ways we cannot yet even perceive; we only know that our mothers were in some incalculable way on our side. But if a mother had deserted us, by dying, or putting us up for adoption, or because life had driven her into alcohol or drugs, chronic depression or madness, if she had been forced to leave us with indifferent, uncaring strangers in order to earn our food money; . . . if she had tried to be a "good mother" according to the demands of the institution and had thereby turned into an anxious, worrying, puritanical keeper of our virginity; or if she had simply left us because she needed to live without a child . . . the child in us, the small female who grew up in a male-controlled world, still feels, at moments, wildly unmothered.[19]

Many well-meaning mothers didn't provide adequate nurturance, protection, or guidance for their daughters because they simply couldn't share what they didn't have. Mothers are first daughters, and they may be living with their own unidentified and untreated Mother Hunger. Every mother is carrying the resources, beliefs, and traumas of her maternal ancestors. And for each woman, "the loss of the daughter to the mother, the mother to the daughter, is the essential female tragedy."[20]

For many reasons, reading this book can be triggering. Identifying Mother Hunger is about healing unmet essential needs now that you are an adult. As you go through the concepts in this book, you may vacillate between feeling angry with your mother and feeling like you're betraying her by reading this. Most of us are trained to be good daughters, and we minimize our mother's behavior no matter how much it hurt. On the other hand, you may want to blame your mother. Blame is a natural stage of grieving and a very normal part of Mother Hunger, but it's a terrible place to get stuck. If you find yourself unable to move past blame, it might be a sign that you need more support for healing this wound.

If you have children of your own, reading this book might be extra challenging. Mothering is not for the faint of heart. While we are biologically wired to nurture and protect children, mothers receive conflicting and contradictory advice that makes the job much harder. You already know what it's like to struggle with guilt because you don't measure up to a manufactured mothering standard. You've had those days when you lost your patience. And your temper. And your mind. You may question why you had children in the first place. These are all normal feelings that come along with the incredible pressures of mothering in a cultural wilderness that doesn't adequately support you.

If your children are older, estranged from you, or struggling in their life, you may feel despair from the loss of closeness with them. But as you gain new insight, remember to stay focused on your experience as a *daughter*. Although I cover principles of mothering, this isn't a parenting manual; I've included this information solely to help you identify what you lost as you grew up to be the person you are today. Healing your Mother Hunger is the purpose here, not an examination of your mothering.

Again, the relationship with *your mother* is why you're with me here. While you recover lost parts of yourself, please don't go to your children, no matter how old they are, to process raw feelings about this material. As your heart heals, your children will inherit the gifts of your labor without any explanation. In the well-crafted words of *My Grandmother's Hands*, Resmaa Menakem, M.S.W., says, "One of the best things each of us can do—not only for ourselves, but also for our children and grandchildren—is to metabolize our pain and heal our trauma."[21] If you are the mother of a daughter, trust that daughters always want their mothers. At almost any stage of life, a new bond is possible—particularly during certain powerful transitions, such as her adolescence or becoming a mother herself, when many daughters once again long for a mother's love and guidance.

For many of you, reading these pages may trigger painful flashbacks to your childhood. If this happens, I encourage you to find a well-trained trauma-sensitive attachment therapist who can help you make sense of disturbing emotions and memories. Healing Mother Hunger doesn't happen in isolation. Mother Hunger is a relational wound that wants relational repair. To avoid getting stuck in despair, it's essential to have a trustworthy guide.

Men, Women, and Mother Hunger

I am often asked whether men, too, can suffer from Mother Hunger. The short answer is yes. All babies need maternal nurturance and protection. If they are missing, both boys and girls experience Mother Hunger. But as boys mature, their need for guidance moves from the mother to the father. Boys typically turn toward the world of men to find mentors and to fit into cultural masculine ideals. For nondominant boys, this process is loaded with complications, but Mother Hunger may not be one of them.

While diverse role models are also helpful to girls' maturation, they specifically benefit from uninterrupted maternal guidance. In fact, it is through their mother's body, mind, and spirit that daughters define femininity, biology, and themselves.

"Good Enough" Mothering

Decades ago, Dr. Donald Winnicott, a British pediatrician and psychoanalyst, gave us the concept of the "good enough" mother. At the same time, he also gave us one of the only working definitions of *mothering*. Winnicott explained that "good enough" mothers tune in to the needs of their newborns. Somehow, "good enough" mothers understand the temporary urgency of a baby's needs. They seem to know that sensitive responsiveness is critical for their newborn's health, and that there is something essentially good about the early bonding processes. Barring other life adversities, "good enough" mothers help build securely attached children who meet developmental milestones because they feel safe and loved.[22]

The term *good enough* makes me uncomfortable. While part of me finds it a relief—a way to think about mothering (or anything else, for that matter) without holding ourselves to an impossible standard—it minimizes the monumental importance of early attachment processes and the critical importance of mothering. Therefore, it's a term I won't be using to explain Mother Hunger.

Three Essential Elements of Mothering

To understand, treat, and write about Mother Hunger, I needed a framework more precise than "good enough" to quantify maternal love. Over time, I identified three essential maternal elements that contribute to a sense of worth and security: nurturance, protection, and guidance. These are the elements of care that translate into maternal love.

Nurturance: A mother is our first source of nurturance. She provides both food and comfort. Her ability to respond to hunger and our need for closeness teaches us about the world from the first moments of life. From her nurturance, we learn whether or not we matter. We learn how love feels.

Protection: Maternal protection is basic to survival. Protection enhances development by buffering threats that would otherwise create fear and anxiety. These threats could include anything from lack of shelter to angry siblings or insensitive adults. Protection begins in utero and continues for a long time, as daughters require maternal protection from forces that devalue and violate girls.

Guidance: As they grow older, daughters watch mothers for cues about what it's like to be a woman. Daughters learn how to treat other women from a mother's respect and care. They learn how to be strong and kind, warm and brave from her example. If the first two elements of nurturance and protection were missing, however, it's unlikely a daughter will trust her mother's guidance. The bond is simply too fragile. Instead, she may break away from her mother's rules, her mother's style, or her mother's wishes.

Mothers who provide these essential elements are a refuge from the storm of life. Of course, even mothers who provide these elements will make plenty of mistakes along the way. Fortunately, mistakes don't create Mother Hunger. Mother Hunger comes from *unacknowledged* damage to nurturance, protection, or guidance. Mothers who recognize their mistakes and make repairs keep bonding secure. In order for any mother to do this well, she must be nurtured by friends, protected by partners, and supported by family. If these resources aren't available, a mother may need professional support in order to meet the demands of mothering.

Mirroring and Empathy

With repetition and predictability, a baby's neural makeup mimics her caregiver's, imprinting a template for how to love and how to feel. Warm, regular touch helps her brain grow, feeding the neurons that promote bonding. A baby develops in her mother's arms, against her mother's heart, one breath at a time. In the mother–infant dyad, the symphony of love orchestrates a brain equipped to master observation, communication, and social connection that will serve her throughout life. Mirroring makes this nonverbal learning possible.

When we smile at someone, their mirror neurons for smiling fire up, stimulating a chemical reaction in their brain that releases dopamine and serotonin, hormones that increase happiness and reduce stress. Likewise, when we see someone smile, it fires up our own mirror neurons for smiling.[23] This is the mirroring principle in action. Mirroring lets us feel or "get" another person. This requires no cognitive effort; it's biologically wired into our mirror neurons. In this way, we automatically feel what someone else is feeling simply by seeing their facial expressions. Mirroring is the beginning of empathy. And empathy makes us human, providing a foundation for connection and community and insulating us from loneliness.

Mirroring begins in the first months of life. All babies study their mother's face. Her eyes, her smile, her facial expressions are clues about whether or not they're safe and loved. If a mother's face looks warm and relaxed, her baby will appreciate the sign that all is well. On the flip side, if a mother looks angry or cold, the infant's mirror neurons register a threat. When a mother's blank face or furrowed brow greets her newborn, human connection can become an unpleasant, even terrifying, experience for a developing baby.

Isolation and Loneliness

In recent interviews, former surgeon general Dr. Vivek Murthy discusses the toxic nature of loneliness. He explains that ongoing loneliness creates a "chronic stress state" that in turn damages the immune system; creates inflammation, heart problems, depression, and anxiety; and increases the likelihood of premature death. "Chronic loneliness is the equivalent of smoking 15 cigarettes a day," according to Dr.

Murthy.[24] In a culture that encourages independence training for babies and children, too many parents are profoundly unaware of their baby's critical attachment needs. Fearful that their children will be weak, needy, or spoiled, the most well-meaning parents make mistakes that leave their little ones lonely, negatively impacting secure attachment and setting the stage for Mother Hunger to grow.

As adults, many of us live with a deep, unconscious craving for love and security that stems from too much loneliness during vulnerable, dynamic periods of brain growth. While we might appear capable and strong, deep within there is a nagging sense of emptiness. Adapting to loneliness too early in life leaves a deep hole where love and connection should have been. We're without an internal compass for love and life, muddling along with brains adapted to loneliness and unprepared for healthy relationships.

First Love

Whether disturbing or validating, a mother's love is your first love, planting the seeds for how you feel about yourself, other people, and the world around you. If your first experience of love is positive, other relationships often are too. If not, broken maternal attachment sets the stage for all other relationships in your life. Whether you felt the burden of caring for her emotional well-being or couldn't get enough of her attention, this fractured connection with the most important person in your life leaves you feeling wrong or bad—and vulnerable to addictive cravings, mood swings, isolation, and shame. Many women share with me how well-meaning friends, spiritual directors, and mental health providers don't understand this pain. In fact, some actively discourage discussing it. It's no wonder that you might feel disloyal or ungrateful if the topic of your mother comes up. When there isn't a safe place to talk about your loss, grief gets stuck in your body. Mother Hunger goes unseen and untreated, and it continues to impact your moods and those you love. Understanding the nature of the first relationship in your life doesn't mean you're ungrateful or feeling sorry for yourself. Think of it as a brave step toward wholeness. *Recognizing what you had and what you lost directs the path toward reclaiming what you need.*

There Is a Name for Your Pain

Living with unidentified Mother Hunger is like going through life with blinders on. You simply can't heal what you can't see. In these pages, we take the emotional blinders off to identify the elements of maternal care that were not part of your upbringing. We will take a deeper look at the three critical elements of mothering so that you understand what happens to development when one or more goes missing. Understanding mothering helps you reclaim what was lost.

Your experience of Mother Hunger is unique to your relationship with your mother, yet the anguish is universal. The emotions that come with Mother Hunger include common human feelings of sadness, anxiety, or confusion. These universal feelings usually find relief in relationships with friends and partners. But Mother Hunger complicates bonding with others, so unfortunately, relationships don't always bring relief. For this reason, it's easy to get stuck. Mother Hunger thrives and endures in a climate of loneliness, fear, and shame. These stressful emotions regularly need addictive relief, which is why, for so many, food, sex, love, work, exercise, or spending can become addictive. We will discuss how this happens in Chapter 4: Surrogate Comfort.

Even though this is a very difficult topic, if you are identifying with and healing from Mother Hunger, I hope this book helps you feel less alone. After reading this chapter, you know there's *a name for your pain*. Critical things were missing from your formative caregiving environment. Years of embedded emotions are going to find their way to the surface now as your body's wisdom takes over. With a name for your heartache, new strength is on the horizon.

CHAPTER 2

ATTACHMENT THEORY AND MOTHER HUNGER

Attachment theory is gaining momentum as the overarching psychological explanation for why humans live and love the way we do.[1] Our individual attachment style is an embodied map for how we connect with others. While human attachment behaviors are diverse, we each have dominant patterns of connecting and relating with others that imprint very early. For purposes of understanding Mother Hunger, we will take a close look at the formative months in our mother's care when we are "learning" to attach.

Dr. Dan Siegel, author, psychiatrist, and director of the Center for Human Development at UCLA, offers a clinical perspective: "Attachment establishes an interpersonal relationship that helps the immature brain [the child's] use the mature functions of the parent's brain to organize its own processes."[2] In the absence of a steady, nurturing, protective adult, early attachment lessons can lead to insecurity. *Mother Hunger* is a term that describes what adult insecure attachment style *feels* like and what happens when essential elements of maternal care are missing. Understanding the root cause of insecure attachment directs healing and increases the possibility for forming secure attachment in adulthood.

Attachment Theory

Attachment theory was born after World War II when John Bowlby, a British psychiatrist and psychoanalyst who worked in orphanages, noted that even though the children were receiving food, shelter, and medical care, they did not thrive; in fact, many died.[3] Bowlby began to study how this could happen, and later Mary Ainsworth expanded on his work. From their research, tested around the world many times since, attachment theory brings us back to a basic truth: human babies are hardwired to depend on caregiver nurturance.[4] Babies are bonding machines, biologically designed to stay close to a primary caregiver. If a baby or child isn't thriving, it may not mean something is wrong with them. Rather, it can be an indication that something is absent in the caregiving environment.

Just as a newborn needs protein and fat to build her brain and body, she needs her mother's warmth to strengthen the social areas of her brain. Cuddling stimulates infant brain growth. So do the thousands of micro-interactions that come with being changed, fed, and carried. Each moment has the potential to build a sense that *people equal pleasure* and that the world is a welcome, safe place to be. Peaceful, responsive interactions between a mother and her baby stimulate the infant brain's reward center, activating dopamine, serotonin, and other neurotransmitters that make life feel good. The more snuggling there is in a baby's world, the more receptive her brain will be to love and other happy feelings as she grows. In the first 18 months of her life, her rapidly growing sensory neurons are silently learning from her mother's responsive proximity.

Healthy maternal care enhances development of the right brain. The right brain is the heart of future commonsense thinking and the ability to read other people's cues and cultivate empathy for how others feel. *Right brain growth depends on predictable, sensitive attachment moments.*[5] Dr. Allan Schore, professor of interpersonal neurobiology at the Geffen School of Medicine at UCLA, calls this an "experience-dependent" process.[6] In this way, a mother's love is the foundation for a brain that fundamentally trusts or mistrusts human connection.

Learning to Attach

Primitive experiences of loving touch and safe sounds are stored in the body as implicit memory. Implicit memory, or body-based memory, is how we hold information about the world and our family before explicit memory, or conscious memory, comes online. Explicit memory lets us recall what happened yesterday, last year, or last night. Our understanding of implicit memory comes from psychologists Peter Graf and Daniel L. Schacter, whose findings illuminate how and why we sometimes react to early experiences without having conscious memories of them.[7] Our cells hold the stories of very early experiences, regardless of how much time has passed. But implicit memory has no recall.

Because portions of our limbic brain, specifically the amygdala where emotions are processed, are functioning at birth, initial human interactions are very important. Even as infants, we capture sensations about the environment (safety, belonging, joy, stress) in our implicit memory. Implicit memory is a primitive part of our innate intelligence, teaching us about safety and love before higher cortical areas of the brain develop and help us understand reality. From the last trimester of pregnancy through a baby's second year of life, the brain doubles in size. During this time of rapid growth, a baby's brain depends on her primary caregiver's brain for emotional regulation—to soothe distress, to feel safe, and to trust human connection. She can't yet "think" for herself. In other words, she needs her caregivers to translate love into baby language through sound, touch, and consistency.

Given the science that informs us that little ones don't have the ability to think like children or adults, it's unfortunate how many misinformed parenting experts teach parents that babies can be manipulative. Manipulation is a higher thinking process that is not yet possible—and won't be for years. Crying or tantrums are not efforts to manipulate caregivers—they are signs of distress and a signal for help. Young, developing children do not have the capacity to regulate emotions by themselves. They learn this from the care they receive.

In essence, babies are sharing a brain with their mothers as they wait for the cognitive brain regions that govern logic and reason to develop. Physical proximity and sensitive interactions with the mother or primary caregiver support the biological processes that allow the brain to develop optimally. When brain hemispheres work well together, learning and regulating emotions is easier. Both aptitudes are entirely dependent on early nurturance and protection, which means that mothers are essentially brain architects. I certainly didn't realize the magnitude of mothering when I was a young mother. This information wasn't available, and I didn't know what I didn't know.

Attachment Patterns

The feelings connected to early care are imprinted in implicit memory. And implicit memory informs our unique attachment-seeking patterns. In this way, our body/mind directs the story of day-to-day life, whether we have awareness of it or not. Lack of awareness and access to these early experiences explains why it's common to think everyone socializes, bonds, plays, or works the same way we do. We may not understand how unique our attachment patterns and behaviors are—until there is conflict with someone we care about. Conflict brings a chance to learn something new about how we bond, what we need, and how others interpret our behaviors. But many of us shy away from the wisdom embedded in conflict because we don't have the tools to understand our own troubling moods or fervent jealousy. We simply don't know *why* we feel the way we do.

The logical part of our brain is missing the key (explicit memory) to early personality formation (implicit memory). When we gain insight into our body's sensations and pay attention to our feelings, we have more control over our choices and behaviors. This process takes time, however, because without explicit memory of our formative months and years, the story of how we learned to attach and to love is not readily available. But be assured that as you learn more about essential elements of maternal care, such as attunement and mirroring, your body/mind may begin to recognize what was lost in your formative years. While recognition

29

may bring difficult emotions, these unpleasant or startling feelings prepare you for healing and transformation.

Attunement

When someone or something is important to you, you give it your full attention. Paying attention is how you demonstrate appreciation, love, or respect. Attention requires both your physical presence and your emotional presence. Attention is attunement. Tuning in to your favorite activity or teacher or friend is a demonstration of what matters to you. Attunement is a full-body expression of your whole self.

Infants who receive attunement from a primary caregiver in the first three years are better able to manage and access a wide range of emotions as they grow and learn. Attachment researchers call these infants *securely attached*. Securely attached children have happy brains. This doesn't mean they are always happy children; it simply means their brains are functioning well.

Attunement is the language of maternal love. Through her gaze, sounds, and touch, a mother teaches her baby how love feels. A baby adores her mother's face. She doesn't care if her mother is brilliant or beautiful, she just wants her to be present. Even if a baby can't yet focus on every detail of her mother's expression, she feels her mother's attunement. Dr. Edward Tronick conducted experiments to illustrate maternal attunement.[8] In his now famous "still face experiment," mothers begin by engaging with their babies in a familiar way. We watch how they enjoy each other, sharing sounds, gestures, and eye contact. After a few minutes, the mothers are instructed to disengage from their babies and keep a still face while staying in the same place.

The mothers stop smiling and making sounds. After only a few moments with a nonresponsive, expressionless mother, the previously joyful babies become confused and distressed. They cry out in protest and strain to get the mother's attention again. Universally, the babies make repeated attempts to reengage with their mothers while the mothers' faces remain blank. The interaction is really difficult to watch. We can see the distress. It's as if the baby is saying, "What happened? Where did you go? What's *wrong*? *I need you!*" Without attunement, a baby can't tolerate her mother's proximity. It is not enough that her mother is physically there; the baby needs her to be emotionally there too.

Fortunately, in the experiment, the mothers make fast repairs (otherwise this would just be cruel) by reaching for their babies, smiling, cooing, and soothing the distress. The live demonstration between mother and baby shows us how powerful the warm dance of attunement is. These early relational lessons are building blocks for secure attachment and future self-worth.

In addition to maternal attunement, we get to see how resilient and adaptable babies are in the still face experiment. With sensitive soothing, they quickly recover from distress. No mother is perfectly attuned to her baby all the time, nor does she need to be. But tuned-in mothers don't let their little ones struggle too long or too often. Like the mothers in the Tronick experiment, they make timely repairs when they miss a cue for connection.

This back-and-forth between a mother and her baby builds trust and secure attachment and is essential for the developing right brain.[9] Current research shows us that by her third month, a baby girl is mimicking her mother's sounds and expressions.[10] And by month four, Beatrice Beebe, Ph.D., clinical professor of psychology at New York State Psychiatric Institute and expert on mother–infant communication, documents that infant girls lose facial gestures that their mothers don't have. Beebe's research has profound implications for a baby girl whose mother is constantly on the phone, distracted with too many other responsibilities, or simply has a flat expression. A mother's facial expressions not only communicate emotions, but they are also creating the brain circuitry for her baby. The quality and presence of the maternal gaze is part of this psychobiological process. So we can understand how lack of maternal attunement is a form of early adversity.

Love Is Not Enough

Love alone is not enough for building secure attachment. And shared DNA is not a guarantee that a child feels loved. Attunement translates love into baby language. In fact, regardless of our age, we all experience love from attunement. We attune to the people who matter to us— or at least we try. Many of us struggle, because attunement doesn't come naturally. If we weren't nurtured this way as children, we need help learning how to tune in to those we care about. This explains the popularity of the mega best-selling book *The Five Love Languages*. In it, author Gary Chapman teaches adults how to express love in ways a partner can feel. Chapman explains that it is not enough to be "in love." We must express love in the language our partner understands. Since this is true for adults, we can understand that it's even more so for infants and children who can't make sense of adult behaviors.

Attunement is the invisible labor of maternal care. Mothers attune in many ways—for instance, by looking for clues that her child needs sleep, nourishment, or soothing. A tuned-in mother observes what calms her baby. A nurturing mother adjusts her touch in ways that her baby likes. She looks for hints that indicate her baby is lonely or scared. A tuned-in mother gives her child space when the little one seems satisfied. These are the powerful yet simple gestures that create a relationship. Attunement is a verb and an active expression of love.

Sometimes caregivers fear that if they respond too often or too quickly to infant cues, they will spoil their baby. But the true meaning of *spoil* is to leave something on a shelf to rot. There is no such thing as spoiling a baby, but this widespread misinformation is everywhere. Tending to a baby's needs for comfort, food, and touch builds belonging, love, and trust. These are essential human needs. When these needs are met at the developmentally appropriate time, later-stage tasks of socialization, learning, and individuating flow. Attunement builds a healthy, robust nervous system that will allow a child to know herself, explore the world, and form happy connections with others in the future.

Secure Attachment

Nurturance and attunement don't have to be perfect for babies to form secure attachment. All mothers make lots of mistakes when caring for their little ones. By holding, rocking, and apologizing, tuned-in mothers make up for natural mistakes. Through sensitive repair efforts like these, mothers reestablish a connection with their children after being away for too long or having an emotional outburst. Nature doesn't require perfection. Children don't either. Secure attachment comes from a relational, dependable back-and-forth between mother and child, implanting the belief that relationships ease pain. These early relational lessons fortify the developing brain systems for ongoing health and happiness and create secure attachment.

Raising a securely attached child is the magic of mothering: an active work of attunement and the monumental choreography of supporting a human being.

Secure attachment allows maturation to flow. Independence is a by-product of healthy dependency needs that have been met during the most vulnerable months and years. Secure attachment is like having a safe place to live, an emotional place to call home. Children with secure attachment tend to be more curious and less aggressive than their insecurely attached peers. They are able to show empathy for others and cope with certain difficulties. Securely attached children go on to form close bonds throughout their life span with friends, lovers, and their own children.

Insecure Attachment

Like anyone, securely attached little ones struggle when bad things happen, but they are quick to bounce back and trust others to help them when things are hard. But infants without adequate early nurturance carry internal distress. Children without secure attachment grow up to be adults with an entire nervous system built differently than those with secure styles. As they physically mature, insecurely attached children have a hard time with emotional maturity. Insecure attachment can lead to symptoms of anxiety. Trusting others is difficult, as is concentration. When kids reach middle school age, insecure attachment may show up as depression, indecisiveness, procrastination, social isolation, disordered eating, or addiction. Attachment science tells us that about 50 percent of the population has an insecure attachment style.[11] *Mother Hunger* is the term that describes what insecure attachment *feels* like—a hunger for belonging, for affection, and for security that doesn't go away despite all kinds of psychological gymnastics.

Signs of Insecure Attachment

For insecurely attached children and adults, emotional distress is more challenging than for those with secure attachment. Missing early nurturance, insecurely attached children and adults struggle to work well with others, withdrawing or isolating when afraid. Insecurely attached people can be excessively dependent and have less patience and flexibility than their securely attached peers. Memory is compromised. Less likely to make long-term friends, insecurely attached people struggle with loneliness. Some can be aggressive during conflict.[12]

The numbers of people with insecure attachment are so significant that it makes absolutely no sense to pathologize this human experience. In fact, insecure attachment could be considered "normal" if we dared use such a word. Psychological adaptations to insecure attachment (mental health issues, addictions, and other health problems) are about lack of support, not moral weakness. Lack of nurturance damages brain circuits meant for connection and strengthens circuits designed for preservation. In this way, insecure attachment is set up for potential, ongoing loneliness. Insecure attachment explains the common experience many of us share—the craving for something or someone to ease the pain of isolation.

Absence of maternal comfort and protection can form an attachment injury before higher functions like explicit memory, cognition, and logic are developed. It's difficult to talk about something that we can't remember. Women with insecure attachment describe feeling heavy, numb, or agitated without knowing why. Struggles with symptoms of depression, dysthymia, or generalized anxiety are common. Third-Degree Mother Hunger (which we will discuss in Chapter 8) shares symptoms with bipolar disorder and borderline personality disorder. Mother Hunger clears up confusion around these symptoms, illuminating the inner heartbreak beneath them.

Women with secure maternal connections can't relate to the despair and shame that go with Mother Hunger. It's not because they aren't well meaning or don't have periods of grief—securely attached women simply don't have Mother Hunger. It is unimaginable to them. They lean into the warmth of their mothers when life is hard, and they celebrate the happy times together. They ask for help when they need it. Securely attached daughters share milestones and other joys with their mothers, whether a marriage, a promotion, a simple recipe, or the birth of a baby. The ongoing interactions between mothers and daughters remain an intimate, formative part of life.

Insecurely attached women, on the other hand, can't relate to warm mother–daughter relationships. They learned very young not to go toward their mothers when they were frightened or sad—and sometimes even when they were happy, because they knew that joy might threaten their emotionally fragile mother. Women recall nicknames that made them feel needy and ashamed, as if they were too much work for their mothers. Some talk about being pushed away when they needed a hug. Others felt overwhelmed with their mother's neediness.

Without healthy maternal nurturance, little girls may grow up with an implicit, embodied sense that *I'm alone, and it's my fault*. Thoughts like these create shame, a self-loathing that gets in the way of self-care, healthy relationships, and genuine moments of joy. Shame feels like a locked cage. Dr. Jean Baker Miller coined the term *condemned isolation* to describe this experience of isolation and shame.[13] Sarah Peyton, author of *Your Resonant Self*, calls it *alarmed aloneness*.[14] The fact that there are multiple names to capture the agony of shame and isolation shows that you are not the only one if you struggle with this pain.

In my years in practice, I have yet to treat a securely attached woman for Mother Hunger. But I have had lots of opportunities to explore the diversity of insecure attachment. Insecure attachment is generally divided into two categories: anxious or avoidant. We will cover both types here. Disorganized attachment, a rich, complex category sometimes called *fearful avoidant attachment*, is often overlooked or misunderstood. For this reason, I will cover disorganized attachment more thoroughly in Chapter 8 as it applies to Third-Degree Mother Hunger.

Attachment style categories are helpful when conceptualizing human behavior, but keep in mind that they were created for research purposes—not to label us. Learning about and understanding the different nuances of attachment is simply for your own awareness. Awareness brings that light-bulb moment when an implicit memory suddenly makes sense and can travel into the part of the brain that gives you access to logic and change. This is how you rewrite a story for healing.

As we review avoidant and anxious attachment, it's helpful to know that no one fits completely in either category. In fact, your attachment style can fluctuate depending on who you are in relationship with.

Avoidant Attachment

Children with avoidant attachment learn to shut down their feelings at a very young age. Most create emotional space from people as a defensive measure—a way to avoid rejection or suffocation. As adults, women with avoidant attachment tend to be linear thinkers. Discussing emotions or feelings makes avoidant folks very nervous. This attachment style is often referred to as *dismissive*, because in the process of shutting down our own feelings, we struggle to relate to how others feel in a genuine way.

I have found two primary ways that avoidant attachment occurs:

Under-mothering: The primary caregiver was frequently unable to respond. She abandoned her child too early and too often, leaving unrepaired separation distress that damaged early bonding. The absence of nurturance required the child to surrender efforts to reach her mother. If no one else came to soothe her distress, the avoidant personality structure began as a way to shut down the need for human comfort and tolerate the intolerable.

Over-mothering: The primary caregiver was suffocating. For infants, over-mothering isn't really an issue. Lots of nurturance is better than not enough. But in time, over-mothered daughters have difficulty getting space from a mother who is engulfing. In clinical circles, we call this phenomenon *enmeshment*. Enmeshment happens when a mother's need for companionship and affirmation overwhelms her child's capacity for autonomy and care. This role reversal asks daughters to nurture the mother instead of the other way around.

Enmeshment is an insidious form of neglect. It is the inverse of nurturance. As teenagers and adults, enmeshed daughters are confused by the anger and frustration they have toward their mothers, who seem so "nice." Therapists might unwittingly coach them to be more patient, turning a blind eye to the heavy burden these daughters are carrying. In this way, anger that an enmeshed daughter feels is ignored and may turn into depression. Without appropriate intervention, these daughters lose validation and don't recognize that their anger is a friend tapping them on the shoulder to notice that something is wrong. We will take a closer look at this type of mother–daughter enmeshment in Chapter 7.

Avoidant women can be very charming initially, giving the impression that they are emotionally present. Generally, this is a learned behavior and not a measure of availability. As adults, avoidant women often feel suffocated or trapped by their closest companions. Distancing behaviors that most of us use with strangers in an elevator or on a subway are default gestures for avoidant women. Unconsciously, their body language and facial expressions communicate *back off* or *leave me alone.*

Women with avoidant attachment easily miss cues for closeness from others and are frustrated when those around them need reassurance, judging them as needy and inferior. Judgment is a psychological adaptation sheltering the tender attachment injury underneath. This self-preservation strategy creates a false sense of power, upsetting the balance in any relationship. Because these avoidant strategies are primitive implicit adaptations to unbearable emotional pain, they are largely unconscious, causing confusion for women when friends or partners point them out.

Since we live in a culture that values independence over interdependence, women with avoidant attachment style are frequently affirmed for their achievements, ambition, and strength. They typically feel more powerful than others. A calm disposition, charming wit, or super-active personality can hide a deep well of insecurity from themselves and anyone close.

Women with an avoidant attachment style are typically attracted to people who are more anxiously attached (and more invested in the relationship) in an unconscious attempt to maintain control and the illusion that everything is okay. This is how they get their needs for closeness met without asking. Asking for connection requires vulnerability, and emotional vulnerability isn't tolerable for women with avoidant attachment.

Avoidantly attached women believe they are actually stronger and more independent than they are. They get bored easily and use their friends and partners to generate energy and activity to keep them engaged. For these reasons, women with avoidant attachment can take a long time to identify Mother Hunger. It generally takes a crisis for an avoidantly attached woman to access her sadness and vulnerability. The threat of a significant loss, such as a relationship that really matters to her or a career opportunity, touches her deep fears of abandonment and causes an avalanche of sorrow that may spur her toward healing.

Anxious Attachment

Unlike avoidantly attached women, women with anxious attachment know something is off with their relational patterns. They typically feel ashamed of their emotional needs. When culture devalues relationships and connection, the anxiously attached woman gets labeled *needy*, *clingy*, or *dependent* as she tries to bond with others. In truth, women who are anxiously attached have cravings for closeness that are hard to satisfy. However, this isn't pathology; it's simply a form of Mother Hunger.

Anxious attachment happens when mothers aren't tuned in to their daughters in predictable ways. Mothers who have difficulty showing affection or have frequent, unexplained mood swings create anxious daughters. Overly rigid and perfectionistic mothers may also create anxious daughters. Mothers who feel overwhelmed by a child's natural needs have facial expressions and body language that may cause a daughter to feel hurt and ashamed, leaving behind the question "am I lovable?"

As adults, anxiously attached women lack the inner structure to be comfortable with themselves and others. They crave closeness with friends and partners but are easily jealous and quick to anger. Adapted to deprivation, they have learned there's a limited love supply. Their emotional intensity sometimes looks like a baby or toddler in a protest state (having a tantrum): crying, screaming, or pouting to bring someone close. Anxiously attached women may rage, pout, starve, or seek revenge when they detect abandonment, even by their daughters.

Women with an anxious attachment style have the same need for autonomy as anyone else, but they don't feel it. For them, being alone is torture and the concept of restorative solitude is unimaginable.

Change Is Possible

Although we each have a dominant attachment style, we can change a bit based on the particular relationship we find ourselves in. For example, even if you are naturally avoidant in relationships, if your best friend needs lots of alone time, you might experience confusion or insecurity

41

with her. Likewise, if you identify with anxious attachment, you might feel suffocated in a relationship with someone else who also has an anxious attachment style.

Regardless of your attachment style, it's very possible to create what researchers call an *earned secure attachment*. In other words, you can change your attachment style. As you restore and reclaim the maternal elements you didn't have, you can build a new sense of security. Healing efforts change neural health and fill in the places where early connection should have been. Just as regular exercise strengthens your body, efforts to restore nurturance, protection, and guidance strengthen your brain. Earned security takes conscious effort, but you are taking the most important step right now: gaining awareness.

Many women earn security with help from a therapist. Some build an inner sense of security with the support of good friends, partners, and even pets. Depending on the severity of your Mother Hunger, the ingredients for enhancing your attachment style will vary. You might be interested in an online version of the Experiences in Close Relationships Scale to take a closer look at your attachment style (openpsychometrics.org/tests/ecr.php). We will take a comprehensive look at what healing looks like in Chapter 9, but helpful practices are included throughout the book.

In the next chapter, we will explore the essential element of maternal nurturance, which has a dramatic impact on how we develop an attachment style and whether or not we know what love feels like.

CHAPTER 3

NURTURANCE

Nurturance is the first essential element that babies need from a primary caregiver in order to build a secure foundation for life. Nurturance is the nonverbal language that tells a newborn *I love you and I'm here.* Merriam-Webster defines *nurture* as "caring for and encouraging the growth or development of someone or something." It comes from the Latin word *nutrire*, which means "to suckle" and "to nourish." I like to think of nurturing as nursing. *Nursing* means tending to the needs of someone who is dependent. Perhaps this explains why we generally associate nurturance with women, because we can breastfeed our infants; however, men can nurture babies too. Both men and women have oxytocin receptors that facilitate bonding behavior.

To understand how Mother Hunger begins, let's look deeper into what *nurturance* means.

- Nurturance is the quality of responsive care between an infant and her primary adult.

- Nurturance is touching, holding, feeding, soothing, grooming, and responding.

- Nurturance is the language of love; the infant brain learns by what it feels.

- Nurturance is critical in the first 1,000 days, when the baby's brain is experiencing the most rapid growth.

- Nurturance is the foundation for secure attachment and brain health.

- Nurturance is basic to all mammals. From the moment of birth, mothers in all shapes and sizes cuddle, lick, nudge, and nurse their young.

At birth, a baby knows her mother's voice and prefers it to all others. While she recognizes other familiar sounds and voices, amniotic fluid has muffled them for nine months. They are the background for the clear connection with her mother's voice. In the first 1,000 days of life, early nurturance from their mother sets up how a newborn's emotional, mental, and physical development will unfold. "The type and process of birthing, close contact with the mother's skin, breastfeeding, and emotional nurturance, protection, and stimulation provided by the family continue these gestational processes beyond birth."[1]

Nurturing Magic

The tender moments and months after birth are so critical that infant experts refer to this as the *fourth trimester*. In the fourth trimester (the three months immediately following childbirth), mom and baby need life to slow down. This tender time should be considered part of pregnancy because the infant brain is growing at an astounding rate—and the fertilizer is maternal nurturance.

For both the mother and the child during first 90 days of infant life outside the womb, eye contact, skin-to-skin touch, and smelling each other intensifies the production of bonding hormones, shaping both their brains. Touch is so important during this time that Yale pediatrician Matthew Grossman, M.D., changed the standard of care he used for babies born dependent on opioids. Instead of treating these babies with morphine and leaving them alone (which is the traditional standard of care and can take weeks), he kept them near the mother, allowing skin-to-skin contact to soothe the withdrawal process. Babies in his care left the hospital sooner than those receiving pharmacologic treatment.[2]

In the months after birth, mom and baby are falling in love. Skin-to-skin contact boosts oxytocin, sometimes known as the love hormone. This is nature's design for human survival. For some, the bond can be instant; for others, it builds gently and gradually over time.[3] Separation between mom and baby is risky during the fourth trimester, or infatuation phase. For the baby, early loss of maternal proximity is encoded as a deep threat. Separation from the mother is the primary cause of newborn stress and may show itself in increased heart rate and blood pressure and decreased oxygen saturation in the blood.[4]

Parents carrying their little ones in slings aren't simply making a fashion statement; they're oxytocin-generating factories. The more touch and proximity between the two, the more oxytocin. Research shows that infants who are touched regularly have bigger, better brains than those who aren't. Oxytocin creates a biological reaction in the mother that can help decrease anxiety and diminishes the need to get busy. Oxytocin helps her want to interact with her infant and meet her needs. Nature designs bonding to feel good and slow us down. Oxytocin floods us during moments like breastfeeding, childbirth, holding, and orgasm. These are moments that are enhanced by stillness, moments designed for bonding. Oxytocin helps couples linger after a sexual encounter. Oxytocin makes mothers want to hold their babies. Oxytocin lets someone else clean the kitchen.[5]

Unfortunately, many people aren't aware of this magnificent hormone or how to maximize it. New mothers who frequently put babies in cribs or bouncers instead of holding them may miss out on nature's magic bonding formula. Well-meaning staff or family who separate mother and baby "so she can rest" are disrupting this critical bonding hormone. Policies that only allow six weeks away from work for a mother are disastrous for the bonding process. Mom and baby need to stay close to each other—in a cocoon of neurohormones—for as long as possible. Much like the first rush of romantic love, newborn infatuation serves a larger purpose: to securely bond these two and set the stage for optimal attachment for the first three years.

A primary caregiver needs a lot of support in the early months and years. In other words, mothers need mothering. Lack of understanding about how much support the primary caregiver needs puts both mother and child at risk. Traditionally, women would have been supported by other women from our communities; however, in the modern world, we tend to live spread out and separated, and this kind of support is rare now. A postpartum doula is one way to buffer this overwhelming period. When a mother has someone devoted to feeding her, caring for other family members and doing the household chores, she can focus on bonding.

In addition to oxytocin, after childbirth a new mother's pituitary gland releases prolactin. Prolactin is the milk production hormone. Each time the baby nurses, nipple stimulation releases prolactin—bringing on intense emotions of love, devotion, and relaxation. Infant suckling also stimulates hormones that give the mother a sense of contentment. In the baby, these same hormones aid digestion.[6]

Babies know how much suckling they need. Sometimes it's about hunger, and other times it's for comfort. For this reason, I like the term *nursing* better than *breastfeeding*. Nursing is nurturing. Nursing includes cuddling, eye contact, rocking, singing, and bottle feeding; anything that keeps oxytocin flowing and allows bonding and attachment to progress.

The science of nursing or breastfeeding is amazing, but make no mistake: it can be hard. Some of the challenges of breastfeeding—plugged milk ducts, lack of support, or difficulty latching on—make it difficult to persevere. Mothers who are able to nurse need time, patience, and support to learn how to tune in to baby-led cues. Feeling pressure to complete other duties or return to work threatens the critical bonding process that mother and baby need.

Learning from Animals

Infant care should be instinctive, but unfortunately, generations of women without adequate nurturance struggle to access nature's design. Modern parenting experts don't help. Many are misguiding parents, suggesting strategies that put babies and children at risk for unnecessary adversity—specifically, too much maternal separation. To counter poor guidance, we can learn much about infant care from studying animals. Researchers and scientists study mice, rats, prairie voles, sheep, monkeys, and other mammals that have brain structures similar to ours to better understand our primal needs for maternal belonging and protection.

Like other mammals, human babies use sound, smell, and touch to identify their mother and prefer her to anyone else. Maternal mammals stay close to their young, clean them, and protect them from harm. Baby animals are not left alone to cry it out unless something terrible has happened to the mother.

Michael J. Meaney's research with mother rats and their pups shows that offspring are heavily influenced by maternal care. When mother rats frequently lick and groom their pups, genes turn on that protect the little animals from future stress. This early maternal protection lasts into adulthood. When babies are deprived of such care, however, the same genes remain dormant.[7] Thus, early maternal care permanently alters brain regions that regulate stress reactivity. Meaney's research mirrors findings from the World Health Organization's review of the importance of early caregivers to infant and child growth and development.[8]

Meaney's research has huge implications for understanding how disturbances in bonding can trickle intergenerationally between mothers and their daughters. He found that early maternal separation hampered the female pups' future ability to nurture their own offspring. Babies of mothers who licked more and nursed more not only showed significantly more capacity to manage stress, but they also nurtured their own babies in the same way. Meaney's conclusions explain why women who feel secure in their mother's love are more likely to have secure infants themselves as well as enjoy stable friendships and romantic relationships throughout life.

Research on what occurs when young children are placed in institutions also provides powerful evidence of the importance of supportive and stable caregiver–child relationships for the health of young children and their cognitive and social development. Young children in group care often fail to thrive; they tend to be sickly, they are demanding of attention, and they find it difficult to have normal peer relationships with other children.[9]

Studies have shown that nurturing touch may be as necessary as food for infant survival. Many of you are likely familiar with Harry Harlow's famous work with rhesus monkeys.[10] Harlow removed baby monkeys from their mothers and divided them into two groups: one group received a wire stand-in mother with a milk bottle. The other group received a soft cloth-covered stand-in mother with a milk bottle. The infants spent more time with the soft mother whether feeding or not. Harlow tried removing the milk bottle from the cloth mother to see if the babies would prefer the wire mother who still offered them milk, but after feeding, the babies returned to the soft surrogate mother. Harlow's study also revealed that infants relied on the soft cloth mothers for comfort. If "she" was there, the baby monkeys were curious and content. When she was removed, however, the little monkeys were paralyzed, huddled in a ball, sucking their thumbs.

Epigenetic Influences

Dr. Rachel Yehuda, director of traumatic stress studies at Mount Sinai Hospital in New York, found that children of Holocaust survivors share post-traumatic stress symptomology with their parents and grandparents.[11] Yehuda also discovered that babies born to mothers who developed PTSD after the World Trade Center attacks shared symptoms of toxic distress, such as being easily disturbed by loud noises and unfamiliar people.[12] As most epigenetic transmission is matrilineal, this research helps us understand how a mother's emotions can find their way to her children. According to Bruce Lipton, Stanford Medical School researcher and scholar, "The mother's emotions, such as fear, anger, love, [and] hope, among others, can biochemically alter the genetic expression of the offspring."[13]

Lipton and Yehuda's research has vast implications for understanding Mother Hunger. Even if your mother very much wanted to be able to nurture, protect, and guide you, her unhealed anxieties or dashed hopes may have left an imprint on your soul. You could be carrying sadness or anger that began with your mother or your grandmother. "When your grandmother was five months pregnant with your mother, the precursor cell of the egg you developed from was already present in your mother's ovaries. This means before your mother was even born, your mother, your grandmother, and the earliest traces of you were all in the same body."[14]

Epigenetics refers to a modification of gene expression rather than a change in the actual genetic code.[15] Culture, diet, and lifestyle can alter gene expression. Gene alterations pass from mother to daughter to granddaughter and adapt to the environment. Since your biological mother was your first environment, if she was stressed, ambivalent, overwhelmed, or carrying her own unhealed trauma, you may have inherited feelings of anxiety and dread before life experience taught you to feel this way.[16]

Nighttime Parenting

Mothers crave their babies for a reason: closeness ensures the best chance of infant survival. This is our mammal brain and body in action. Babies who don't get enough time with their primary caregiver are vulnerable. In the succinct words of Erica Komisar, "Our denial of the very specific and special physical and emotional role of a mother and her child, particularly in our attempt to be modern, is not in the best interest of children and their needs."[17]

Mothers are bombarded with misguided advice about infant and young children's needs, especially sleep. For an infant or toddler, falling asleep is a moment of separation and must be understood this way. Infants have not changed since we were hunting and gathering, but our modern world somehow expects babies to sleep alone in cribs for extended hours. Only recently, the science that supports keeping mom and baby close during sleep is gaining recognition.[18] We are learning, or relearning, about infant sleep and how normal it is for babies to wake frequently. They are designed to feel the nearness of the mother's body in order to feel calm and avoid unnecessary hormones that the body releases when it senses danger. Breastfed babies benefit from frequent feedings throughout the night, so the closer they are to mom, the easier it is for both.

To a baby, separation from the mother's body means danger. Too many parents don't realize how damaging hours of separation can be for dependent newborns.[19] Erica Komisar explains in detail the benefits for both mother and child to sleep close to one another (in the same room or bed, within sensory recognition of each other) for up to six months or a year. Komisar says that nighttime security is even more important than daytime security—especially when a mother has been gone all day.[20]

In his book *Nighttime Parenting*, Dr. William Sears explains how and why babies sleep differently than adults. Little ones are designed for survival, so they wake easily to co-regulate themselves with their mother. Sears explains that infants who wake up alone feel startled as they search for their mother. Increased adrenaline and heart rate lead to crying and difficulty going back to sleep. Sears explains that infants who co-sleep rarely cry during the night and have less nighttime anxiety. As adults, they experience fewer sleep disturbances than adults who slept alone as infants.

With the exception of children whose caregivers abuse alcohol and nicotine, babies build a robust physiology through closeness with their parents during the night. For example, since newborns cannot regulate their own body temperature, babies who co-sleep have more stable body temperatures. Additionally, carbon dioxide exhaled by the parent stimulates a baby's breathing patterns, and infants sleeping near their mothers have fewer pauses in breathing compared to babies who sleep alone. Both Dr. James McKenna, infant sleep researcher at Notre Dame and author of *Safe Infant Sleep: Expert Answers to Your Cosleeping Questions*, and Dr. Sears point to low incidence of sudden infant death syndrome in countries where co-sleeping is the norm.[21]

Dr. McKenna points to 45 to 60 million years of primate evolution and suggests that current "Euro-American infant care practices, and our infant's ability to accommodate these practices . . . suggest that we are pushing infant adaptability (and indeed maternal adaptability) too far, with deleterious consequences for short-term survival and long-term health."[22] Dr. McKenna explains that recommendations from authorities who claim that co-sleeping is unsafe are based on the few parents who irresponsibly handle nighttime care for their babies. This is like saying that because a few people can't manage their credit cards, no one should be allowed to have a credit card. In his opinion, committed, careful parents are disregarded when sleep recommendations are made. Dr. McKenna's guidelines state that room sharing can be a safe, simple form of co-sleeping, because primary caregiver and baby stay within sensory range of each other.[23] "This form of co-sleeping is safe for all families and would be, in my mind, the preferred and default sleeping arrangement especially for non-breastfeeding infants."[24]

Clearly, the physical and social conditions surrounding infants and caregivers determine how risky or beneficial co-sleeping is and what kind of co-sleeping to try (emphasis on *try*, because learning how everyone gets a good night's sleep is a process that takes creativity and experimentation). Many experts agree that sharing sleep space benefits the bonding process, which could explain why Dr. Sears has found that parents who embrace nighttime parenting create children with higher self-esteem, less anxiety, ease with affection, and increased independence.

Birth

Childbirth is a profound experience for a woman, opening a psychic portal into deeper parts of herself. If her own early experiences with her biological mother were positive, feelings of joy may flood her body and brain as she brings forth new life. She is psychologically and biologically ready for bonding.

Just the opposite may happen for a woman who experienced inadequate or harmful early care. When a woman gives birth, the amygdala (the brain area responsible for regulating fear response and stress) naturally lights up. It comes online and stays online to keep a mother alert to her baby's needs. For women with untreated Mother Hunger who are already overly alert, this increased amygdala response can set off a cascade of panic during the early bonding months, severely compromising maternal mental health. Vulnerable and raw, these women tend toward elevated sensations of loneliness, despair, and boredom in the early days with their newborns. Dark emotions and hypervigilance interfere with bonding and unveil the story of a mother's own early moments of life.

Childbirth itself can also be traumatic for mothers and babies. In hospitals, nurturance may get derailed by a medical emergency that requires early separation between mother and baby. Feeding difficulties are likely when this happens, and that adds stress to an already vulnerable time. A detailed exploration of birth trauma is beyond the scope of our conversation, but I will note that postpartum distress intensifies when birth and delivery are traumatic.

Additionally, postpartum distress can escalate when a new mother is estranged from her own mother or has a mother who is unsupportive or no longer living. In these cases, the most important source of comfort during this rite of passage is lost. In my opinion, unidentified and untreated Mother Hunger may be a leading cause of postpartum depression and anxiety.

Separation

During the three months following pregnancy, mothers experience intense emotions that come with lactation, recovery from childbirth, and all the many changes of motherhood. One of the best remedies for maternal anxiety and distress during this time is physical proximity with her infant. Close skin-to-skin contact boosts hormones that soothe and regulate both mom and baby, buffering their anxiety and stress. Mothers separated from their infants miss out on critical skin contact that increases milk supply and promotes relaxation.

Extra care and support are essential for both babies and mothers during this time so they can spend as much time together as possible. The competing needs of other children, financial pressures, work schedules, medical emergencies, and unsupportive partners may require too much separation between a mother and her newborn, interfering with early bonding and ongoing attachment needs and creating lifelong physical and psychological consequences for both.

What constitutes too much separation? Erica Komisar has interesting insights about mother–infant separations:

> The most painful times for young children are the comings and goings of their mothers. Babies need security, consistency, and predictability from their mothers, especially during times of transition, such as waking up; going down for and waking up from a nap; moving to and from daycare or preschool; and switching from playtime to bath time, from bath time to dinnertime, and from dinnertime to bedtime.[25]

The dominant culture assigns a higher value to work outside the home than to mothering, leaving women torn when it comes to how best to have both. It's not uncommon for mothers to feel confused about priorities, how to manage time away from their children, and even how to make their children proud. This is completely understandable, but it's important to keep the early years out of this thought process. Little ones just want their mothers' presence. They don't care about her résumé.

It's safe to say that separations that regularly create infant distress are problematic. Nothing prepares an infant for the isolation of a crib when she's used to the sound of her mother's heartbeat. Babies don't understand that mom needs to go on a business trip or that she promised dad a date night. When a baby is separated from her mother for too long, unless there is a nurturing, familiar caregiver to take her place, the primitive brain registers a threat. And the infant brain learns from what it feels. A baby without her mother may feel a threatening loss that jump-starts her nervous system by releasing adrenaline. Crying, shaking, or screaming are signs of a distressed baby with too much adrenaline in her system; this is an infant in a fight-or-flight state. Fight-or-flight hormones are not meant for babies. But extended separations from familiar arms will initiate these powerful neurochemicals.

It is a travesty of medicine that some experts warn parents that crying babies are being manipulative. Ignorance like this may account for the widespread number of adults with insecure attachment. "The most natural way that we humans calm down our distress is by being touched, hugged, and rocked. This . . . makes us feel intact, safe, protected, and in charge."[26] Encouraging parents to leave babies and children alone to self-soothe defies nature's design. We are created for connection. Self-soothing is an advanced skill that comes later and flows naturally after bonding is secure. When mothers and caregivers embrace the power of nurturance and the essential timing of the early years, their emotional and physical presence builds secure attachment and fills the space where Mother Hunger might grow.

Reclaiming Nurturance

You can start healing touch deprivation anytime you're ready. Imagine the way you would have liked your mother to touch you as a child. Would she stroke your hair? Maybe scratch your back? Maybe you would have liked her to sit quietly near your feet or by your side. You can practice warm self-touch to soothe and reclaim lost maternal nurturance.

I find Reiki useful to start with, especially when you aren't sure about doing something like this. If your own touch is overstimulating, try gentle movement with a lightweight scalp massager or dry brush until you feel more comfortable with regular self-nurturance.

Here's a Reiki practice to try at night when you get in bed or when you have time and space that feels safe.

To begin, sit or lie down and rub your hands together until you feel the warmth that comes from the energy inside you. Wait for a tingling sensation. When you have it, place both hands at the crown of your head, lightly hovering over or touching your skull. Wait there while the tingling falls like rain over your head. Enjoy the sensation. Notice the warmth at the crown of your head.

When the warmth in your hands cools, rub them together again and hover your palms over your closed eyes. With your hands lightly touching each other, place one hand over each eye. Feel the warmth. Is it stronger than at the crown of your head or less so? When the energy cools, move on to the neck and throat area. Notice how your neck responds to the warmth of your hands. Do you feel any emotions bubbling up?

It can feel awkward to not know exactly where to place your hands. Don't worry . . . this is a practice; it doesn't need to be perfect. If you are a visual learner, there is a helpful diagram put out by the Cleveland Clinic illustrating the sequence of Reiki positions.

You can continue down your spine, laying your hands over your abdomen and then your pelvis, noticing the emotions that come from each chakra as you pay attention to yourself. You may want to cry. You might feel calm. You may fall asleep before you finish. Notice if you get irritated or bored with this exercise. Collect the information. Keep trying self-touch in small doses when you can. With time and practice, you can change your body's response to touch and reduce your cravings for unhealthy substitutes.

CHAPTER 4

SURROGATE COMFORT

What happens when maternal care is unavailable or compromised? Missing maternal care demands a substitute—someone who can take over as the primary caregiver. When a sensitive and reliable alternate caregiver is available, such as a partner, a full-time nanny, or a grandparent, infants and toddlers can benefit from relational security even when their mothers aren't available. But if an adult who can meet the needs for nurturance and protection is not available, resilient little ones must cope with distressing changes that come with life outside the womb on their own. They find other ways to feel secure even when they aren't. They soothe themselves. They find surrogates for missing maternal love. In the words of Tara Brach, meditation teacher, author, and psychologist, "When we have unmet needs, we're wired to meet them in another way."[1] Most of the time, the personality and behavioral adaptations that fill in for compromised mothering happen so young that no one notices. Leading busy lives, well-meaning parents may miss the signs that their babies are learning to distrust human connection.

What Is a "Good" Baby?

Babies who don't cry or fuss are often called "good" babies. "Good" babies sleep through the night and don't bother their caregivers. I feel sad when I hear parents speak this way. Sleep patterns have nothing to do with being a "good" or "bad" baby. Infant cries aren't signs of poor character. Biology fuels crying to bring a caregiver close—babies cry because this is how they communicate. Communication is central to bonding. And bonding is core to survival.

While some babies are born with a peaceful or quiet temperament, the idea that a "good" baby is a quiet baby is uninformed and unkind. Expecting a baby to sleep a full night without needing her mother is an unfortunate misunderstanding of infant development and parental responsiveness. While many newborns sleep a lot in the first four to six weeks, most will fuss and cry more as they acclimate to life outside the womb and need more support to fall asleep. Babies aren't designed to sleep like adults. It's natural for them to wake frequently for food or comfort. Without any training, babies fall asleep when they are tired. Sleep, like hunger, is natural.

When a baby is hungry or lonely, she cries. While crying, she experiences a rapid increase in heartbeat and release of adrenaline.[2] Adrenaline, or epinephrine, helps start nature's fight-or-flight response. In adults, this looks like driving to a restaurant, foraging in the refrigerator, or calling a friend to talk. In babies, it looks like crying.[3] Nature prompts us for action with powerful neurochemicals. A responsive mother brings relief before her baby gets too elevated. If not, infant protest efforts increase. She starts to cry louder. This is biology in action, not a willful baby.

Babies without sensitive, responsive nurturance may eventually stop crying when they need something. Constant crying is too hard on a vulnerable little body. Crying cessation is an example of adapting to compromised care. So, it's possible that a quiet baby might be a resigned baby. Infants who experience a routine lack of responsiveness—as in the case of sleep training that separates an infant from her mother or uses the "cry-it-out" method—will eventually stop crying. Sleep training may certainly teach a baby to be quiet, but it has nothing to do with attachment—or nurturance. Nurturance, the most primitive human need for healthy development, requires responsive, sensitive care so that human connection feels natural and development is optimal. Nurturance and sleep training are not compatible. Isolating a baby to put her to sleep is the opposite of nurturance.

Sleep training experts argue that infants can self-soothe, but they demonstrate a profound lack of neurobiological accuracy. This is such harmful information for new parents who are trying to do the right thing for their little ones. Infants can't self-soothe. Self-soothing is a sophisticated higher function that develops much later in life. In fact, most adults can't self-soothe. And why do adults who prefer sleeping with a partner expect a baby to sleep alone?

Anything that looks like self-soothing, such as thumb sucking, is purely *auto-regulation*, a scientific term for coping with isolation. Self-soothing, or auto-regulation, is what we do in a pinch. It's not designed to be a substitute for a relationship. And sleep trainers also don't tell parents how to stop their little ones' self-soothing behaviors in a kind, respectful way when it's time. Experts don't alert parents that they will need to step up nurturance efforts when they take away the self-soothing object or try to stop the auto-regulating behavior.

I have so many painful examples from grown women who remember how they were shamed for sucking their thumb when it was time to go to school. I've learned how common it is for women to keep their first baby blanket or stuffed animal—if they are able to. Often parents hide or throw away these early attachment substitutes in an attempt to make their child more independent—which is simply uninformed and heartbreaking—and leaves a deep mark of mistrust. Countless times, I hear women share the story they were told by Mom or Dad: "I don't know what happened to your teddy" (or blanket or doll). But they felt it was a lie. The simmering hurt and anger is still very much alive decades later as they share the memory of loss.

Expecting a baby to self-soothe may have more to do with parents needing a break or cultural expectations for American parents than baby's well-being. This is under-standable. Infant care is challenging, frustrating, and hard, so while taking a shortcut makes sense, it may backfire. Iso-lation to train a baby to go to sleep puts incredible pres-sure on the developing nervous system that needs human connection for comfort. Too much "self-soothing" sets up a need for other auto-regulatory substitutes (sugar, alcohol, fantasy, sex) as a child grows up, because she is learning that she must meet her own needs instead of resting in the com-fort of her caregiver.

When separation happens too often and too long, the infant's body understands that things are really bad, and the freeze response, designed to buffer pain and fear, takes over. The freeze response is a step down the brain stem from protest efforts like crying or screaming. When this lower system is engaged, the baby gets quiet and sleepy. Breathing slows down. Her body may sag, and she may appear visibly resigned. A freeze response might look like a "good" baby, but it is really a baby learning to give up. She is learning that her needs won't be met, that human connection can't be trusted. This painful lesson won't unfold well as she gains maturity.

Mother Hunger Begins

When we are helpless infants, hunger pains drive us toward our mother. She is our relief. Completely dependent on her care, we "talk" to her with our whole body—we squirm or whimper or cry. This is nature's way of bringing Mom close. When she responds with milk and warmth, all is well. Milk and mother bring pleasure, and we learn that a full belly, our mother's touch, her voice, and her smell are the same. This is how human connection gets associated with pleasure so that we want more of it. Hunger and bonding are inextricably biologically linked.

Categorically, women with Mother Hunger struggle with both food and relationships. I have never seen one problem without the other. It's just a matter of which hurts more. From early nurturance experiences, food and love become linked in implicit memory. Think of the last time you were really hungry. What did it feel like? How long could you tolerate hunger pains before you got something to eat? Hunger hurts. The pain comes out of nowhere. From deep inside, a place you can't see, hunger pains get your attention. Adrenaline prompts you into action, so you find food.

If hunger cries were often ignored during your infancy or toddler years, or your mom didn't enjoy feeding you, or the others who fed you didn't really know how, the pleasure of bonding was compromised. Warm satisfaction and pleasure may be linked for you with the physical sensation of fullness, but not with human contact. Food brings relief from pain, but a relationship doesn't. This is how we fall in love with food.

Inadequate Nurturance

Josie was put in her big sister's bedroom right after she was born. Her big sister was only 10 years old, but it was her job to mix the formula, heat the bottles, and feed Josie throughout the night. While a big sister might enjoy this for a night or two, a 10-year-old is still a child who needs sleep. A 10-year-old can't substitute for a mother.

"Do you know why was this your sister's job?" I asked Josie.

She wasn't sure. "I was the last of six, so maybe Mom and Dad didn't want me."

There it is—the implicit belief a child creates when maternal nurturance is inadequate: *I'm not wanted.* This belief becomes part of her internal, unconscious love map that will guide her life and self-image.

In Geneen Roth's transformative book *When Food Is Love,* she states that "many of us have been using food to replace love for so many years that . . . we wouldn't recognize love if it knocked us over."[4] Roth links the powerful connection between food and love that is intrinsic to Mother Hunger. This connection is so strong not because food is actually love, but because it's our first *experience* of love. When maternal nurturance is compromised, food provides the first sense of real comfort. Food rescues a hungry heart. Perhaps this explains why, for many of us, eating is much more than a simple response to being hungry. We eat when we're lonely, stressed, or afraid. We eat when we're bored, tired, or ashamed. Eating rituals are windows into the soul. If you want to know yourself more deeply, notice how and when you eat.

Women with Mother Hunger are conflicted about eating because maternal deprivation required substitute comfort. Some avoid meals and restrict calories to feel strong, visible, or safe. Starving is one of the most basic ways to compensate for feeling helpless. Others are more inclined to overindulge, following the inner voice promising that pizza will make everything okay. Overeating and undereating are effective ways to mask internal distress and numb the void where maternal nurturance fell short.

Eating as Language

Hunger is a human experience. So are hunger pains. Women without maternal nurturance grow up hungry for both love and food and frequently confuse the two. In fact, loneliness triggers brain cravings similar to physical hunger.[5] I look at maladaptive eating habits as signals of wordless despair. Eating patterns tell the story of early attachment, so I pay attention.

Staci Sprout, clinician and author of *Naked in Public*, beautifully captures how she found a surrogate for missing maternal nurturance: "Food became my comfort, my pleasure, and my stand-in for affection and touch. Touch on the inside, touch I could control."[6] Staci's words reflect the way food becomes a primary relationship, standing in for maternal care. Similarly, in the powerful memoir *Hunger*, Roxane Gay discusses the connection between food and love. She shares how visiting her family triggers powerful cravings for food: "I am so much more than hungry when I am home. I am starving. I am an animal. I am desperate to be fed."[7] For so many of the women I work with, returning home stirs up longing, anger, and hunger. It's as if being close to Mom again reminds the body of rejection and longing. Gay says, "I start to crave foods, any foods. I get uncontrollable urges to binge, to satisfy the growing ache, to fill the hollowness of feeling alone around people who are supposed to love me."[8]

Escape Act

Nadine was often frightened as a little girl. She grew up in a home with two parents and an older brother. Her father was always angry. Her brother was a bully, and her mother was too distracted to pay attention. Nadine remembers mealtimes as particularly miserable. She remembers her father criticizing her mother and the food. At the table, he preferred silence. If anyone spoke, his anger became aggressive. Nadine's brother usually provoked a fight, and her mother often left the table in tears. Nadine just wished everyone would be quiet so her father wouldn't get mad at her brother or make her mother cry. To cope with distress, she focused on her plate. She kept her eyes on the food.

When I asked her to remember how the food tasted, she said, "I liked it. If I tried hard enough, I could almost forget anyone was there." Nadine was a resourceful little girl—she found a way to soothe her fear. Focusing on eating calmed her nervous system. But over time, this practice became somewhat automatic. In essence, Nadine learned to isolate herself into a food trance—a zone where nothing else existed except the food on her plate.

Nadine's strategy for regulating fear followed her into adulthood. As a mother now herself, Nadine still prefers to eat alone. She prepares her food and takes it to her room. Her children eat alone in their rooms with computers and phones for company, and her husband does the same. Food and technology replace human connection in this family, mimicking the isolation of Nadine's original home.

Food is a powerfully effective way to regulate emotions when human connection can't. In my experience, helping women rearrange the primitive food bond that serves as a stand-in for early maternal care takes incredible respect and time. This makes sense if we understand that overeating and undereating are in fact related to the fight-or-flight response—a way to escape pain. Unable to leave the family table, or caught with a secret sugar supply, some girls discover very young that food provides a virtual escape from intolerable feelings. Food plans generally don't work because rules feel like deprivation and trigger the primary loss.

We know that food and nurturance are connected. When a friend is sick, we offer food. To celebrate a holiday or accomplishment, we share a meal. But lack of early nurturance distorts the connection between food and bonding, leading to what Alexandra Katehakis, Ph.D., calls the "comfort-without-contact strategy."[9] Comfort without contact, or self-soothing, is what babies learn when there is too much maternal deprivation. This is why sleep training is so risky and can be a setup for Mother Hunger to grow. As a child matures, food replaces thumb sucking or finger chewing.

Food Trance

Maladaptive eating becomes a non-relational habit that fills in for inadequate maternal nurturance. Restricting or overindulging is about longing: a longing to be cherished and safe. Both eating habits are forms of the fight-or-flight response. Without a sense of safety and belonging, fear is ever present, so undereating and overeating are ways to numb fear when there is nowhere to go. When food replaces maternal care, self-development may stop. Hidden beneath the urge to eat or starve is a little one waiting for love and protection.

As well-practiced adults, women eat or restrict food in a mild trance, without any awareness of their childhood fear fueling the food bond. Maladaptive food patterns may continue as if they belong to someone else. Here's how one client, Debbie, experienced it: "In the middle of the night, a different part of me comes out. She crawls into the kitchen, stuffs herself with anything she can find, and goes back to bed. In the morning, I feel sick and puffy. And sometimes I can't remember why . . . until I go into the kitchen and find the mess." For Debbie, late-night eating happens as if she is in a trance. Currently separated from her spouse of 32 years, she is living alone for the first time in her life. At night, unhealed childhood fears wake her up from nightmares, sweating and shaking. Together, we've been exploring how this happens.

Debbie grew up with a needy mother who could be very cold and critical. Debbie did everything she could to please her, but it never seemed to be enough. One moment, she was her mother's best friend, and the next, she somehow made her mad. Never sure why, she remembers the torture of her mother's punitive, stony silence that seemed to last for days. As a little girl, Debbie spent hours alone in her room, hiding under the covers, waiting to be forgiven for whatever she had done wrong. And she ate. She kept a secret stash of crackers, chocolate, and gummies in her closet behind a raincoat, where no one ever looked. It was her own pharmacy.

Now, at age 54, Debbie feels the same desperation she experienced as a little girl. She is losing her marriage, has few friends, and worries constantly about her children and grandchildren. But she explains to me that her biggest source of pain is her relationship with food and how much she hates her body. "I will never be happy until I lose weight. It's the only thing that really matters. I think about it all day, every day." Debbie's internal warfare makes sense to me. It's easier to fight with food than face Mother Hunger.

Like many adult women, Debbie designed her life to please her mother. She went to the school her mother chose. She married the man her mother wanted her to, and she stayed in her mother's hometown. When Debbie had her own children, she trained them to behave so her mother would be proud. And still, her mother was unhappy. As a dutiful daughter, Debbie never got angry with her mother. Instead, she ate.

Debbie's treatment with me began a year after her mother died, which is very common. Facing this work is sometimes impossible with a living mother. Currently, Debbie is coming to terms with the depth of sadness and anger she feels about her life. Although her mother is no longer living, Debbie still feels like a bad girl. Her whole body reacts as if she is betraying her mother by telling me about her childhood. Her face flushes; she squirms and looks away. These are normal reactions many women experience as they remember maternal deprivation and begin to tell the truth. When Debbie shares about eating and body hatred, I'm reminded of Geneen Roth's words: "We treat our bodies as if they are the enemy . . . as if deprivation, punishment and shame lead to change."[10] The change Debbie needs is not really about food. As Mother Hunger heals and her core wound is addressed, Debbie is naturally losing the weight that made her body uncomfortable. As she faces grief, receives support, and replaces lost maternal care, her body is becoming her home.

At the end of this chapter is a questionnaire that makes the connection between nurturance, food, and love more concrete. The rest of this book will be more meaningful if you take a few minutes to write your responses. If this feels too difficult, trust that and wait until you are with a safe friend or your therapist to do this exercise.

Nurturance through Touch

Babies need maternal affection the way plants need water: without it, they wilt. If mom is not nurturing, resourceful infants and girls find other ways to meet this primal need. Little girls are comfort-seeking missiles, and if they are lucky, they cuddle safely with siblings, other mothers, fathers, grandparents, stuffed animals, and pets—someone or something warm and soft.

As a little girl, Caroline's mother would not let her have a stuffed animal to sleep with. "I hated nighttime. It was too dark. I was so scared. She wouldn't let me have a nightlight or a stuffed animal because she said it would make me too needy." Caroline's mother, like many misguided parents, was afraid of making her daughter too dependent. But forcing a child to be independent is futile. It simply doesn't work. Independence grows from a secure, safe maternal connection. Caroline didn't have this. She remembers the loneliness of her bed and her longing for comfort. She sucked her thumb. She stroked her pillow. She fantasized about being rescued.

In *Being There*, Erica Komisar writes about the importance of transitional objects: "Respect your child's needs for blankets, stuffed animals, and/or pacifiers which represent you and the security you provide in your absence. . . . If your child naturally takes to a transitional object, it will be easier for you to leave for short periods of time."[11]

Touch Deprivation

Lack of maternal nurturance leads to touch deprivation. Touch deprivation has a mind of its own. Before girls who lack maternal nurturance get older and have access to drugs and alcohol to comfort their touch-starved bodies, they touch themselves. Before they starve or binge or purge, they touch each other. Before they cut, burn, or bang, they meet their desperate needs with siblings, pets, or anything warm and soft.

Little girls without maternal affection are especially vulnerable to those who might take advantage of them. They don't recognize inappropriate touch, because it's better than no touch. In this way, early sexual abuse may go decades without discovery. Filled with shame, women tell me stories of how they didn't mind sitting on an uncle's lap or touching a grandfather's penis. Even though they knew something was wrong, they rubbed up against their brothers or sisters. Or mattresses, chairs, and tables. Like food, orgasm medicates emotional starvation.

Caroline's mother sent her away to summer camp when she was very young. "I hated the bugs, the lake, and the slimy, awful food. It was like a bad dream." Caroline remembers her summers craving grape soda and Snickers bars. And touch. "I stared at the girls who had long, pretty hair and seemed so confident. I wanted to be just like them. To make them like me, I did anything. Sometimes, we would sneak into an empty cabin. We kissed and touched each other. It was amazing. I never wanted it to stop."

I hear stories like this often. Young girls curling up in the dark refuge of sleepovers, privately exploring each other, grasping for affection before daylight returns and brings them back to their cold, rejecting mothers. Erotic affection between girls often has little to do with sexual orientation and frequently stems from touch deprivation. We are resourceful creatures, and one way or another, as we grow and develop, we find ways to meet essential human needs.

Almost no one talks about girls and masturbation, yet this is one of the first and strongest substitutes little ones find to replace a mother's touch. Self-stimulation, like thumb sucking, is a resourceful way to regulate fear when you're hungry for comfort.

Unwanted Touch

Not all maternal touch feels good. When mom's touch is icky (sexual) or intrusive (aggressive), it's tragic. To cope, daughters shut down the desire for human closeness. The shutdown response isn't a decision. It's a body-based reaction to violation.

Mothers bathe, feed, dress, and undress their daughters. These intimate moments teach a little girl about her body and her worth. When maternal touch is disrespectful in any way, it leaves a lasting impact.

In her book *A Mother's Touch*, Julie Brand writes about being molested by her mother. She recalls naptimes and how it felt strange to have her mother in bed, touching her body. But there was no force or physical pain. When I work with women who share similar backgrounds, they describe their mother's touch as icky or heavy, but they don't identify it as abuse, particularly when it didn't hurt, but also because a mother's touch is "normal" or familiar.

When daughters experience inappropriate touch from their mothers, shame keeps them silent. As adults, these women feel very little desire to be close to their mothers. Driven by duty, they may remain helpful, loyal, and close, but relief comes when their mother dies. Relief is not the same thing as healing. Without intervention, these women may unconsciously repeat a mother's touch with unhealthy partners and self-injury.

When women speak of sexual abuse, the perpetrator is usually a male family member. Dr. Christiane Northrup's groundbreaking book *Women's Bodies, Women's Wisdom* linked father–daughter sexual abuse with future sex and love addiction. Similarly, in *Women, Sex, and Addiction*, author and therapist Charlotte Davis Kasl connected sexual abuse to addictive love and sex. Like Northrup, Kasl points to men. "The role fathers play in the development of female sex addiction cannot be overstated. Little girls take their cues from their dads. They want that special energy, the light in Daddy's eyes, to be directed toward them. The ache for a warm and affectionate dad who did not sexualize the relationship is deeply etched in the hearts of most women."[12]

While I agree with Kasl that a little girl wants to feel special to her father, her assertion that girls take their cues from dad reflects a blindness to the primacy of the mother–daughter relationship. If a daughter is nurtured, protected, and guided by her mother, she's less vulnerable to her father's unhealthy behaviors. And she may not need as much of his time or encouragement. His love is a bonus, but she's already steady from her mother's love. Kasl seems to recognize this herself later in the book as she writes about her obsession with a lover, Sam. "I knew that my attraction to Sam had reawakened the part of me that still felt terribly wounded by my mother."[13] Kasl's process reflects what I've seen happen over and over again. Identifying maternal neglect or abuse doesn't happen until later in life. It's as if we are protected from knowing until we are truly ready to know. Perhaps getting angry with a father for our difficulties is easier than pointing to Mom because our culture allows us to identify men as abusive before women. Or maybe it's even more primitive than that. Psychologically, it might be more threatening to lose a mother's approval than a father's. Most certainly, it's a mix of these complicated factors.

Intimacy Intolerance

Painful, shameful, or nonexistent maternal touch may lead to touch aversion in close adult relationships. Women talk about having automatic responses to romantic partners that seem to come from nowhere—like an allergic reaction. I call this involuntary reaction *intimacy intolerance*. When someone gets too close, intimacy intolerance causes you to feel a little sick. Their emotional proximity feels disgusting or irritating. In *Naked in Public*, Staci Sprout does a remarkable job of describing intimacy intolerance: "I usually hated touching other people. . . . Whenever I tried it, I felt an odd prickly sensation and an urgent impulse to jerk my hand away." For Staci, touching someone created a "sour-hot feeling" that covered an "ever-yawning, excruciating maw of need."[14]

If the concept of intimacy intolerance resonates for you, it may be that you feel hungry for a certain type of love but are mystified by what keeps you from having it. Maybe you find solace in fantasy—the chemical changes in your body that come with imagining a perfect lover are enough. If you go toward relationships, you may be drawn to avoidant partners or friends, because they won't threaten your unconscious intimacy threshold. For you, avoidant partners and friends are better than people who suffocate you.

Hunger Questionnaire

As a child, were you encouraged to eat when you weren't hungry? Were you forced to eat food that was disgusting to you?

_____

_____

As a child, were you deprived of food when you were hungry? Were favorite foods withheld from you?

_____

_____

How were mealtimes in your family? Who cooked? Did you eat together or alone?

_____

_____

As a child or adolescent, did you ever sneak food? Binge? Restrict?

_____

_____

How do you know when you're hungry? What sensations emerge?

_____

_____

What is your favorite food? Why?

_____

_____

Use three words to describe how you feel about food.

- _____

- _____

- _____

Use three words to describe how you feel about sexual intimacy.

- _____

- _____

- _____

Now, look at the words you listed for food and for sexual intimacy. Are they the same? Are they different? Why?

_____

_____

CHAPTER 5

TOXIC WATERS

Mother Hunger doesn't arise in a vacuum. Mother Hunger is created and transmitted within a culture that obscures our human need for one another and prioritizes men over women. Mother Hunger is part of a much bigger picture that frightens women and compromises our ability to protect ourselves and our daughters. Before we talk about the essential maternal element of protection, we need to take a look at the cultural context that makes it difficult for a mother to keep her daughter safe.

Protection is a positive human attribute that ensures the survival of a species. Symbolically and literally, maternal love represents protection, standing between a child and life's hardships. A child can endure many threats if she knows her mother is there for her. The term *mama bear* speaks to the universal protective instinct wired into female physiology that is activated when a woman becomes a mother. Designed to ensure the survival of the next generation, mothers experience increased neurochemical activity that enhances attention and proximity seeking. Maternal protection is part of nature's plan to keep infants and children safe while they are too vulnerable to protect themselves.

Unfortunately, cultural influences can obscure nature's design. What kind of world makes it difficult for a mother to protect her child? The answer to this question involves a discussion of patriarchy, from the Greek meaning "rule of the father."

I've been writing and teaching about patriarchy, misogyny, and the construction of gender for 30 years. So when I stumbled on Anjali Dayal's interview on the radio show *On Being*, I was thrilled with her fresh, clear explanation. Dayal, at the time a research fellow at Georgetown University's Institute for Women, Peace and Security, shared David Foster Wallace's graduation speech "This Is Water" to make a point. In Wallace's anecdote, two young fish swimming along meet an older fish who calls out, "Morning, boys. How's the water?" The two young fish continue swimming for a bit before one of them looks at the other and says, "What the hell is water?"[1] The meaning is clear: we're often wholly unaware of the environment that shapes us. Dayal brilliantly connects this "water" with patriarchy:

> Patriarchy is evident in the everyday violence against women. It is reflected in the battlements we build to protect ourselves: the little accommodations, the things you do reflexively to keep yourself from being hurt while you walk around, all the subtle ways you protect yourself from being alone with some men in offices and other men in cars and all unknown men in large empty buildings . . . every time you've ignored the lewd comment from a man on the street or at a bar or at a party, because who knows what he'll do if you lash out . . . the quick scan of a subway car when the train pulls into the

station to ensure that there are enough people so you won't be alone if someone threatens you, but not so many people that you'll get groped without being able to place the hands—a thousand transgressions so small and so regular that you never name them to anyone . . . because *that's just the way life is.*[2]

The psychobiological, social, and spiritual impact of growing up in patriarchal water means we swallow mainstream ideas about women without realizing it. Even when these ideas are damaging, we as women become versions of the gender stereotype. The way the culture looks at us is the way we see ourselves. The way the culture feels about us is the way we feel about ourselves. Internalizing patriarchal ideology isn't a cognitive process. We don't consciously wake up one day and decide to devalue ourselves. It's much more insidious. We simply swim in feminine constructs that tell us how to behave, how to look, and who to love as we grow and develop. And sometimes we learn this from our mothers.

Cultural Factors That Contribute to Mother Hunger

Growing awareness of the "mother wound"—a matrilineal burden that manifests in women and is passed on from generation to generation—gives us the framework for understanding the origin of Mother Hunger. Mothers carrying their own victimization pass it on to their daughters. Self-loathing and contempt corrupt the mother–daughter bond as hatred of women is shared. "A mother's victimization does not merely humiliate her, it mutilates her daughter, who watches her for clues as to what it means to be a woman. Like the traditional foot-bound Chinese woman, she passes on her affliction. The mother's self-hatred and low expectations are binding rags for the psyche of the daughter."[3]

Dr. Oscar Serrallach describes the transmission of the mother wound by explaining the cultural forces that require women "to internalize the dysfunctional coping mechanisms learned by previous generations of women." Serrallach describes the mother wound as "the pain and grief that grow in a woman as she tries to explore and understand her power and potential in a society that doesn't make room for it."[4]

Mother Hunger, in part, is a legacy of the mother wound. Passed from grandmother to mother to daughter, the belief that women are somehow less than men damages our bond with each other as we pass our internalized beliefs about our body, worth, and power to the next generation. The unconscious and epigenetic processes that teach us to be "feminine" occur without our consent.

Many of us struggle with body shame and limiting beliefs—lessons from our mothers. We watched our mothers starve. We witnessed their boredom and anxiety. We saw them betray their friends and themselves. As a result, many of us have no idea how or why we struggle; to us it is simply "normal."

#MeToo

It seems each decade brings fresh attempts to reverse toxic masculinity and rebalance power between men and women. Toxic masculinity is built on a false belief in the superiority of men. While it might appear that certain men (white, heterosexual men) benefit from this setup, in truth, toxic masculinity is damaging to men too, because the rules of what a man can feel, how he can behave, or what he must achieve force limited access to feelings and vulnerability—the very qualities a man needs to connect with his partner, his children, and himself.

In 1975, Laura Mulvey taught us about the male gaze—the way we collectively view women as objects—in her famous essay "Visual Pleasure and Narrative Cinema."[5] Through media, collectively, we learn that women exist for the visual pleasure of men; but since we all look at the same things, women learn to see ourselves and each other this way: as objects. Renee Engeln, psychology professor at Northwestern University, identifies the enduring quality of the male gaze, explaining how the female body "is seen as something that exists just to make other people happy."[6] The male gaze teaches us that to be visible, we must be groomed, thin, and young; we must tease, flirt, and exhibit ourselves. Paradoxically, visibility makes us vulnerable. Feminists in the U.S. coined the term *rape culture* in the 1970s to describe a society where sexual violence is normalized and victims are blamed for sexual harassment and assault. Rape culture emphasizes "don't get raped" instead of "don't rape."[7] Emilie Buchwald, Pamela Fletcher, and Martha Roth, editors of *Transforming a Rape Culture*, describe rape culture as:

> a complex system of beliefs that encourages male aggression and supports violence against women. It is a society where violence is seen as sexy and sexuality as violent. In rape culture, women perceive a continuum of threatened violence that ranges from sexual remarks to sexual touching to rape itself.[8]

The 24-hour news cycle includes so much coverage of this continuum that violence against women seems unavoidable. The #MeToo movement reminds us that in spite of all the years of hard work and waiting for things to change, a woman can still be pinned to a bed, cornered at a party, or groped while others stand by and watch. Women intuit that even if the news isn't about our story specifically, it could be. A culture of fear permeates the female psyche, complicating our ability to keep ourselves and our children safe—compromising the essential maternal element of protection.

Pornography

Easy access to pornography adds difficulty for parents who want to protect their children. Pornography flourishes in rape culture, and it is now available 24/7 on handheld devices. As a result, children are seeing pornography more than ever before. A recent British survey found that 12 percent of children under age 12 regularly watch pornography.[9] While pornography can be a helpful way for adults to explore disenfranchised parts of sexual preferences and dreams, when children accidentally find pornography, it can be terrifying. Mix fear and arousal and the brain is overwhelmed.

While advocates fight to protect children from the adverse impact of pornography, a generation of kids are growing up learning about sex from porn in spite of their mothers' protective efforts. Pornography as sex education is problematic for many reasons, which include but aren't limited to a deep misunderstanding about gender, sexuality, power, and emotional intimacy. Gail Dines, author of *Pornland* and president and CEO of Culture Reframed, sees the widespread infiltration of pornography as a public health crisis. She describes our modern rape culture as "pornified culture" and explains how porn creates boys with less empathy and more likelihood of sexual aggression.[10]

Sexual Alarm

Women acquire biological adaptations to endure constant threat. We are braced for danger with a regular dose of adrenaline and cortisol. As we grow, our personality develops in a type of defense mode. Defense mode may explain why some of us are angry, loud, and aggressive while others are furtive, hypervigilant, and withdrawn. Judith Leavitt, in her book *The Sexual Alarm System*, explains how women are so accustomed to sexual fear that—without our awareness—our bodies are constantly on guard, like a low-level hum. Leavitt calls this adaptation the *sexual alarm system* (SAS). The SAS keeps us on high alert, preparing us for "the possibility of abuse," because we know it's possible and "we are alert and watching out for it. Otherwise, we would go out for a walk anywhere at any time of night, or travel freely anywhere in the world, or not worry about the men on the street following us."[11]

The SAS blares out at women to WATCH OUT. They are prey! They then go through becoming wired, getting triggered, going on high alert, and finally withdrawing and shutting down. Whew! This is stressful and exhausting. And it affects many aspects of women's lives! Most men do not experience the SAS because they are not, in fact, sexual prey.[12]

A personality of defense starts early. From a young age, we learn we aren't safe because our body is an object that can be sexually exploited and violated. The sexual alarm system is a product of patriarchal culture.

Constantly Guarded

The instincts that drive us to appease someone who has real or perceived power over us diminish our chances for full relational participation. Thus, many of us have never experienced a healthy romantic partnership, because relational reciprocity is a foreign experience. Toward our own protection, we "appease and please" someone else's needs for food, sex, adoration, or even money. The need to appease someone with power (perceived or real) is our biological freeze response in action—our adaptation to chronic, ongoing fear.

Female bodies in patriarchy are adapted to danger. According to Dr. Shelly Taylor, women respond differently to danger than men do. In her groundbreaking work, now widely known as the tend-and-befriend theory, Taylor found that women demonstrate more social behaviors in response to a threat.[13] Prior to her study, published in 2000, we assumed that the only biological response to fear was either fight or flight. Our information was based on male physiology. Taylor's research focused on women instead of men and set out to explore other ways we respond to danger. Her theory posits that fighting or fleeing are less advantageous for women who have babies and children depending on them. Women are therefore more at risk than males in terms of injury or dislocation when someone or something is dangerous. For this reason, she found that women "tend" (cook for, groom, or stroke their offspring) and "befriend" (gather, talk, connect with other women) when frightened.

In another study examining gender differences, a group of men and women were informed that they would experience an electric shock. In the course of the experiment, women chose to wait for the shock with other participants while the men dispersed and waited alone.[14]

The tend-and-befriend theory makes sense when we think about how women have better chances of survival when they stick together—as do their children.[15] What accounts for this difference in fear response between men and women? It is undetermined whether it's biology or sociology, but for understanding Mother Hunger, the distinction isn't critical. In fact, I think different fear responses may relate to our attachment style as much as to gender. Regardless, Taylor's theory helps us appreciate the power of the sexual alarm system and why we may appease, tend, or befriend rather than flee when threatened.

Appeasing with a Purpose

A deeper understanding of our human fear response allows more compassion for ourselves when some of us unconsciously appease an angry partner before soothing or protecting children; our mind rapidly determines, at some deep level where automatic survival resources kick in, that soothing an angry adult is the safest option for everyone.

Marissa Korbel, staff attorney at the Victim Rights Law Center and monthly contributor for the Rumpus, gives us a powerful illustration of appeasing in action. In her article titled "Sometimes You Make Your Rapist Breakfast: Inside the Controversial—and Often Confusing—'Tending Instinct' of Women," she writes:

> You can only push a man off you so many times. You can only say "not now, no thanks, I don't want to" so many ways. I, too, have had sex I didn't want because sex was the least bad option. Sex was a known variable. Think of it as a harm reduction tactic. Fighting and screaming and kicking and yelling at a man? Unknown outcomes. Would he hit me

back? Would he let me go? Would I fight and lose? If I lost, would he have sex with me anyway, only more violently?[16]

Korbel captures the essence of the appeasing response. Appeasing behavior may be less risky than fighting or running. So we can understand how surrendering to unwanted sexual aggression is about survival—a resourceful, preconscious harm-reduction tactic.

As children, many of us learn to appease our mother as a harm-reduction tactic. Rather than risk an angry mother, appeasing her meant we kept the house clean, complimented her appearance, kept her company, or stayed out of her way when she was irritated. Pleasing and appeasing is similar to a trauma response—it's an automatic, unconscious reaction that can become an engrained personality trait.

CHAPTER 6

PROTECTION

Frightened women make insecure mothers who sometimes fail to protect their children. This isn't a matter of love. Mothers may fiercely love their babies and children and still be unable to protect them. I see these patterns a lot in everyday life as mothers try to raise their daughters. Some mothers are overly protective and daughters miss out on developmentally suitable experiences. On the other hand, some mothers are so permissive that daughters face adult challenges before they are ready. The right balance is mysterious. And it's complicated by unhealed trauma that follows a woman into motherhood. Unaware of her own psychological wounds, a mother may miss the cues that she is in danger and so are her children. Or it seems that danger is around every corner, leaving both mother and daughter on edge. Either way, daughters struggle when they can't count on their mothers for safety and protection.

Early lessons in safety and security between mother and daughter may not be measurable or visible, but they are powerful. Beginning with pregnancy, scientists are learning, maternal anxiety, stress, and fear can be passed on to a baby in utero, specifically in the last trimester.[1] Additionally, a mother's unrepaired emotional scars from her own upbringing adversely impact her maternal instincts.[2] Maternal stress and anxiety pass insecurity to a daughter through touch, vocal tones, and breathing patterns, and later through behaviors and choices that put both mother and daughter in harm's way.

To illustrate the concept of maternal protection and how it can go wrong, it's helpful to look at extremes so that we might notice more commonplace examples that happened in our own upbringing. For this reason, I will focus on the Netflix series *Dirty John* based on the true-life story and original podcast. You might find it helpful to watch or listen to the series to gain a full understanding of the dynamics at play.

The Case of Dirty John

In the Netflix adaptation of the true crime podcast *Dirty John*, we have a brilliant but dark illustration of what happens when mothers cannot protect themselves or their daughters. The miniseries illustrates how intergenerational transmission of misogyny can leave women unsafe and vulnerable. Misogyny is not just overt hatred of women, but also, according to the Cambridge Dictionary, "the belief that men are better than women."

In this true-life story, we see firsthand the legacy of damaging double standards that prioritize men over women—and how women participate in and perpetuate this unfortunate system. Three generations are impacted by systemic misogyny transmitted with the help of Judeo-Christian ideology.

The intergenerational transmission begins with Arlane, who is the wife of a pastor. In a poignant, painful scene, Arlane quotes scripture to her grown daughter Cindi to encourage her to stay in an unhappy marriage. Like most grown daughters, Cindi wants her mother's support. She is considering divorce, which is daunting as a Christian woman. Life transitions that don't have cultural support are hard, and maternal love makes things easier. Cindi listens as Arlane quotes scripture, advising her to stay in her marriage to Billy. Cindi ignores her own intuition in order to please her mother and be a "good" Christian daughter, but soon after, in a chilling display of calculated malice, Billy murders Cindi. Although Billy goes to jail for manslaughter, he is released after only three years, based on Arlane's testimony that "I know he loved my daughter." While compassion and forgiveness are admirable, something in Arlane's twisted tolerance for her son-in-law doesn't sit well. As the story unfolds, we see how Arlane's guidance is a tragic display of systemic misogyny that overrides the protective maternal instinct.

Arlane and Cindi are backdrops to the main character in Netflix's dramatized series, Debra Newell, played expertly by Connie Britton. Debra is a 59-year-old woman who is successful in business but chronically disappointed in love. Debra, like her sister, Cindi, is a magnet for dangerous men. As the story begins, we witness Debra being easily seduced by John Meehan, played by Eric Bana. Debra has been married and divorced four times, yet her track record doesn't seem to slow her down when she starts online dating and finds John. John quickly works his way into her life. The audience can see John's predatory strategy through the concerned eyes of Debra's grown daughters. Within weeks, Debra secretly marries John despite her daughters' protests, and their relationship shows hallmark symptoms of love addiction.

Love addiction, like any other addiction, follows certain criteria that indicate when a habit has become a compulsion:

- *Continuing behavior or substance use despite negative consequences.* Debra is unable to stop seeing John despite uncovering his lies and experiencing loss of closeness with her daughters.

- *Trying to stop a behavior or substance use without success.* Debra tries to stop seeing John after discovering his dark motives, but she can't. As her obsession grows, she is increasingly unable to care for herself and lies to her daughters, putting them in grave danger.

- *Craving and withdrawal when trying to stop a behavior or substance use.* Debra breaks up with John after first learning about his deception, drug addiction, and history of deceiving other women. However, she can't tolerate the separation and reestablishes contact with him.

- *Keeping the behavior or substance use a secret.* Debra lies about her relationship with John from the very beginning. She lies about how fast things are moving, how much access she is giving him to her personal life, and how much of her finances are compromised. She hides getting married. She hides these details from her family so that she can be with John.

- *Isolating from friends and family to protect the relationship.* Debra has no female friends, and she withdraws from family relationships as she prioritizes John.

Despite Debra's prior divorces, neither she nor her mother, Arlane, seem cautious when John quickly becomes part of daily life and holiday traditions. Both mother and daughter show no ability or inclination to slow down and get to know him before including him in family life. They are seduced by his charm. But Debra's daughters are not.

The eldest, Ronnie, is clearly haunted by her mother's four previous marriages. Her rage is overt. She keeps a large metal safe in her closet where she protects her valuables, and she shuns her mother's new romance with John. Ronnie, unapologetic in her defensive posture, is the protector. She has adopted the parental role that her mother has abandoned.

Debra's younger daughter, Terra, is disturbed by the relationship but shows her fear in very different ways from her older sister. Unlike Ronnie, Terra tries to appease her mother. She pleads with Debra not to allow John to play with the younger cousins during the upcoming Christmas gathering, tearfully explaining that it's not fair for kids to get attached to a man who won't stay. Terra can't directly ask her mother to stop seeing John (like Ronnie can), so she tries to appeal to her mother's heart.

In her tender, utterly reasonable request, we see Terra's heartache; she knows the pain of repetitive loss. We wonder what it's been like for her to bond with each previous stepfather only to have him leave, or to wait behind a new man to have her mother's attention. She wants her mother to understand—to protect her and her children from further, unnecessary loss—but her pleas are futile.

The role of mother as protector is so misunderstood that even professional intervention misses Terra's desperation. The therapist fails to hold Debra accountable, and ultimately, Debra's love addiction wins. She disregards Terra's request and allows John to make dramatic gestures with

Christmas gifts for the small cousins. Watching the scene, we know this isn't the first time she's turned a blind eye to her daughter's needs to meet her own.

Sometimes women compensate for misogyny by behaving like those in power—they offend someone more vulnerable. In the case of Dirty John, Debra's disregard for Terra's simple request is an example of how this may happen. Debra ignores her daughter's plea for protection. Instead of listening and considering her daughter's needs, Debra puts her own desires before her daughter's well-being. Shamelessly, she allows John to shower the young cousins with toys and affection. And when Terra has an emotional reaction to her mother's poor choice, Debra is angry and hurt. She feels victimized by her daughter's behavior and goes so far as to apologize to John for her daughter's "rudeness."

But the true victim in this holiday moment is Terra, who is alone, crying, in a back room, trying to make sense of things by herself. To make matters worse, Arlane tries to smooth things over by cajoling Terra to rejoin the holiday gathering instead of listening to her concerns or asking John to leave. Both mother and grandmother prioritize John over Terra, sending the clear message that his needs are more important than hers. More than anything, Terra wants to please her mother, so she wipes her tears, blows her nose, and returns to the party. To have her mother's love, she sacrifices her intuition and her needs. Ultimately, in an unthinkable turn of events, she almost sacrifices her life. John tries to kill her. Watching this story come to life is horrifying on so many levels, and I couldn't help but think of Cindi dying at the hands of her husband while witnessing Terra fighting for her life. Debra's failure to protect Terra might seem like an extreme form of neglect, but it highlights the generational nature of women unable to protect each another from systemic sexism. *This* is how Mother Hunger happens.

Sisters with Mother Hunger

When a mother is unable to protect her daughters, not only do siblings miss out on maternal protection, but their personality adaptations also make them competitors for whatever love is available. Unprotected children grow up guarding themselves and fighting for attention. As a result, when siblings most need an ally, they frequently end up with an enemy—or, at the very least, a difficult relationship laced with competition and resentment.

In the case of Dirty John, we see how, without maternal protection, daughters adapt by taking care of themselves the best they can. Ronnie and Terra, each fierce in her own way, make extraordinary efforts to preserve a connection with their mother. Ronnie hires an investigator to save her from John, and Terra tirelessly turns to Debra for comfort and understanding. As they each strive for maternal love, their relationship with each other becomes tenuous.

I've seen this pattern of sibling tension over and over again in cases of Mother Hunger. Many sisters become adversaries as they individually survive a mother who acts like a child. When siblings strive to survive, they don't play. They rarely relax. One becomes parental; the other stays young. Siblings take on roles like peacemaker or comedian. Sometimes children just hide from the chaos, quietly retreating into themselves.

While the Netflix drama adeptly illustrates Debra's inability to protect herself and her daughters, reviewers miss the point—and miss an opportunity to educate. Perpetuating the idea that children are "bad" when they are defiant or oppositional, Heather Schwedel in *Slate*'s culture newsletter refers to Terra and Ronnie as "full of sass" and lazy.[3] Schwedel grossly minimizes the emotional struggle that Terra and Ronnie have endured. Using disparaging language, Schwedel's description perpetuates the cultural habit of victim blaming. Her assertations that the sisters are "bratty adolescents" completely overlooks the reason why these girls behave the way they do: they are afraid. A new man with their mother is a threat. They know, without really knowing, that they are in danger because their mother cannot and will not protect them.

Vulnerable Mothers Make Vulnerable Daughters

Ideally, maternal protection implants an internal source of security in a daughter. But it doesn't always work this way. The story of Dirty John may seem extreme, but it is not unique. Generations of women have sacrificed the well-being of their children while tending to male partners.

We see this between Debra Newell and her girls. She treats her daughters as decorations, wanting them at family gatherings but irritated by their routine daily needs. Though she's unable to see or respect her daughters' feelings, she feels victimized when they can't respect hers. In an interview, real-life Debra says, "I thought [John] was after me for my money, so I didn't feel that my kids should be in fear."[4] Debra's words show a willful disregard for her daughters' thoughts and feelings. She is blind to the danger she puts them in. Although Judeo-Christian theology calls us to "honor thy father and mother," sometimes it is impossible— and indeed unwise—to "honor thy mother."

Neuroception

Mothers who don't protect their daughters fall into two categories: the mother who is too vulnerable and the mother who is threatening. In this chapter, we will discuss the first type: the vulnerable mother. (We will take a closer look at the impact of threatening mothers in Chapter 8: Third-Degree Mother Hunger.) When a mother has unrepaired attachment injuries from her own upbringing, her capacity to soothe herself or her daughter is compromised. An emotionally fragile mother may have facial expressions that frighten her daughter or vocal tones that are hard to listen to. Easily distressed, a vulnerable mother can't tolerate it when her daughter has big emotions, particularly if they are negative emotions. Afraid that she has no solution, a vulnerable mother may push her daughter away to avoid feeling helpless.

Neuroception, a term from Stephen Porges's polyvagal theory, is the brain's ability to distinguish the meaning of others' moods and behaviors and to pick up on and understand environmental cues.[5] Neuroception helps us determine whether someone is safe or dangerous. An anxious mother who is routinely afraid may adversely impact her daughter's developing neuroception that is linking up with her own. Daughters match, or co-regulate, with their mothers. In this way, anxiety between mothers and daughters is shared.

Through the thousands of tiny gestures between mother and infant, mothers communicate whether or not the world is safe. Adaptations to a mother's fear can inhibit a daughter's ability to play, learn, and feel comfortable making friends. Feeling anxious, she loses access to her inner wisdom and intuition. In the most extreme cases, a daughter may lose the ability to detect danger altogether. She will miss cues that signal that someone or something is a bad idea. When maternal neuroception is damaged, sometimes mothers and daughters end up in danger—as in the case of *Dirty John*, where Terra ultimately fights John for her life and Cindi marries a man who kills her. Damaged neuroception helps us understand how a tragedy like this can happen.

Earned Protection

Inside each adult woman who did not have early maternal protection is a frightened little girl. Usually her anxiety is firmly packed down under layers of defensiveness. I call this defensiveness *earned protection*. Earned protection manifests in many different ways. Some girls are fierce. They have rapid movements, forceful voices, and frequent demands. Displays of dominance alert others to back off and be careful. On the other end of the spectrum, some girls appear submissive or compliant, their posture bent or unsteady. They may rely on others to make decisions for them.

If you meet a woman who has buried this type of Mother Hunger under fierce defenses, you might not know she is afraid. Externally, she might seem strong. But underneath a carefully crafted veneer, her frozen personality parts wait for attention. One part is a frightened little girl who longs for maternal protection. Another part is an angry teenager who had to figure things out by herself. Unaware of these parts, a woman who did not have early maternal protection may find herself attracted to powerful authority figures who have status and wealth or she may work tirelessly and ferociously to build her own financial fortress. She is seeking the protection she didn't have as a child.

Although a woman carrying this type of Mother Hunger can take care of herself, she is tired of doing it. She longs for someone to take control and relieve her of responsibility, someone to let her be the little girl she never got to be.

Women who grow up without maternal protection are accustomed to high levels of fear and anxiety. If this is part of your story, you have been living with high levels of stress and self-management for a long time. Your endurance may be running thin. Because maternal protection was missing, you adapted very young, and part of you may still feel like a frightened girl at times.

Loving Isn't the Same as Protecting

Too often, hard to soothe infants are called "difficult" babies, and distressed toddlers get misguided labels like "terrible twos." Little ones who cry are seen as manipulative or oppositional when they are simply communicating the only way they know how. Blaming young children for primitive emotions is a missed opportunity for attunement and connection.

Relationally dependent, babies and toddlers can't manufacture a feeling of safety by themselves. Just like a fragile tree that needs additional support when first planted in the ground, infants are supported by their primary caregiver. When a plant isn't thriving in the garden, we don't blame the plant. We test the soil. We monitor the sunlight. We adjust the water. We work to enhance the environment so the plant can thrive. But with children, sometimes we have this turned around—we expect a new baby to adapt to the environment, even if she's clearly not doing well in it. Instead of turning away or feeling persecuted, a tuned-in mother might ask herself, *What does my baby need?* and strive to soothe her little one. Protective mothers apply sunscreen, wash the vegetables, and call the doctor. And these are the easy tasks.

When we're frightened, our awareness changes, our voice changes, and we stop smiling. The micromovements in our face get tight. Fear can cloud a mother's capacity to pay attention to her infant's cues or be present when her toddler is feeling afraid. Sarah Peyton, author of *Your Resonant Self*, explains this phenomenon, saying, "Because fear takes people out of presence and into vigilance, it also moves them out of being able to pay attention to the nuances of what is happening for someone else."[6] What if that "someone else" is a baby?

Most women I know keep the doors locked when we're home alone, have our keys ready as we walk to the car, and avoid parking garages after dark. It's scary living in a world where we are sexual prey. Frightened mothers can communicate that danger is near without language. Researchers at the University of California–San Francisco found that infants "catch" the psychological residue of their mothers' anxiety and distress.[7] As we discussed in the mirroring section in Chapter 1, we know that by four months of age a baby has already learned her mother's facial expressions. Babies regulate their nervous system in sync with their mothers'. In this way, maternal distress can become infant distress.

No Safe Haven

Generational and environmental adversity compromises a woman's ability to protect herself and any children she may have. In the words of Dr. Gabor Maté, "We are not talking about individual parental failure. We are talking about a broad social phenomenon. We live in a society . . . that completely destroys the parenting environment."[8] The social phenomenon Maté refers to is the patriarchal water we're all swimming in that devalues our human vulnerabilities and need for one another. This social phenomenon damages maternal protection.

When mothers struggle for safety, so do their children. Daughters of frightened mothers search for protection where there isn't any. "[When] the immature stress response goes without nurturing protection from a stable adult . . . such adversity leads to psychological trauma."[9] Mothers in danger are unable to buffer their little ones from toxic stress. Toxic stress activates the immature immune system and can alter genetic makeup, leading to lifelong challenges with mental and physical health.

We are just now appreciating the magnitude and consequences of childhood adversity thanks to widespread awareness of Vincent Felitti's landmark adverse childhood experiences (ACEs) study, published in 1998 by the Centers for Disease Control and Prevention and Kaiser Permanente.[10]

The original study of ACEs specified 10 categories of stressful or traumatic childhood events, but the list has now been expanded to include many more. Forms of childhood adversity include racism, parental incarceration, acrimonious parental separations, having an addicted parent, living in foster care, and witnessing a mother being threatened. With over 17,000 participants, the study shows us that sustained stress during childhood causes biochemical changes in the brain and body, drastically increasing the risk of future mental illness and health problems, including substance abuse.

Interestingly, and not as commonly known, Dr. Vincent Felitti first discovered the link between childhood adversity (specifically sexual abuse) and adult mental health problems accidentally. A patient participating in his highly acclaimed weight-loss program revealed her childhood trauma during an interview, sparking a powerful moment for Dr. Felitti, who had never before asked about childhood abuse while treating patients for weight loss. When asked why he had never made this connection, he replied that he was a medical doctor, not a therapist.[11] What a powerful example of how and why medical training should include trauma awareness education.

The ACEs study shows a common denominator in each measure of adversity: a lack of protection. Children without a protective caregiver suffer more than children who have one. Dr. Robert Block, former president of the American Academy of Pediatrics, is often quoted as saying, "ACEs are the single greatest unaddressed public health threat facing our nation today." Growing awareness of ACEs and their consequences reveal how much children need the protective presence of a consistent caregiver. Research shows that if a trusted adult soothes a child during adversity, the impact of distress is less damaging, and the event may not become an ACE. One pediatrician is taking this very seriously: Dr. Nadine Burke Harris, the first surgeon general of California and author of *The Deepest Well*, is connecting the dots between childhood illnesses and toxic stress and making changes to medical procedures that could further traumatize vulnerable children.[12] In her widely viewed TED talk, Dr. Burke Harris says, "The single most important thing that we need today is the courage to look this problem in the face and say, this is real."[13] Childhood trauma isn't something you just get over as you grow up. (For more information about ACEs, see "ACEs Science 101" and "Got Your ACE Score?" at ACEsConnection.com.)

Protection in the First Three Years

The most accurate predictor of a securely attached child is protective, sensitive caregiving during the first three years.

In preparation for birth, women need support and awareness to optimize relaxation and avoid unnecessary distress.

In the early months of a newborn's life, biological processes are profoundly impacted by safety or lack of safety. At about six weeks gestation, the placenta connects mother to daughter. When a mother experiences fear, the cortisol released in her bloodstream crosses unfiltered to her baby. In this way, anxiety may first be experienced in utero. If you are reading this sentence with an "aha" feeling, perhaps anxiety that has been with you for a long time is making new sense.

Newborn bodies and brains have not adjusted to relatively modern parenting arrangements that separate babies from their mothers for a long workday, a vacation, 10 hours of sleep, or even a medical emergency. Such separation would have been unheard of for our ancestors, who lived closer to the earth. And if you were born and raised during a time when experts encouraged the cry-it-out method, it's safe to say that you adapted to fear very early.

In the Nurturance chapter, we talked about how risky mother–infant separation is for attachment success. It bears repeating again in this chapter. Separation is scary for infants and hard on mothers for a reason: survival. A mother who must leave her little one knows on some level that this may adversely impact her child, so she may struggle to focus or work or enjoy time away.

"Secure attachment makes separation less painful for children, but separation causes a child pain even when that child has an emotionally present mother," Dr. Komisar writes.[14] I love her emphasis on the pain that children feel when mom goes away *even if* they are securely attached. Komisar normalizes the primacy of the first relationship we all have in life.

Studies show that children under the age of three who are in daycare have higher levels of cortisol in their saliva than children at home with familiar care.[15] These studies reveal that as many as 63 percent of kids in daycare have raised cortisol levels, which is associated with delayed development and immature brains in four species of mammals (cattle, sheep, rats, and monkeys). High levels of cortisol have been associated with brain changes that lead to a continuing elevated stress response.[16] While little ones benefit from socialization in daycare and preschool, they aren't psychologically or emotionally equipped for peer interactions before they are two years old.[17] Peer play goes more smoothly when early attachment needs have been met. Attachment must precede socialization, not the other way around.

As a mother and clinician, I'm not surprised by Komisar's findings about ADHD and other behavior problems: "I have seen society increasingly devalue mothering while idealizing work. At the same time, I have seen an epidemic of troubled children who are being diagnosed and medicated earlier and earlier with ADHD, early aggression, and other behavioral and social disorders. Many people say these two phenomena are utterly unrelated. I believe they are connected."[18]

Little ones depend on their relationship with their mother to soothe anxiety and stress that comes with new experiences. The security of this relationship is the basis for attachment and feelings of safety. Secure attachment happens gradually as trust grows in connection with predictable, warm care. If you didn't have a sense of safety growing up, the separation anxiety that is evident in little ones might still be with you. You might feel a deep uneasiness when you are alone or when someone leaves.

Many argue that encouraging mothers and infants to stay in close connection for the first 1,000 days is somehow anti-feminist. But this couldn't be further from the truth. Feminism is about *expanding* choices for women. Having more choices comes with more responsibility.

The choices we make have rewards and consequences. We make better decisions when we have comprehensive information. Many women would make different choices about mothering if infant care experts and authorities were providing holistic information and supporting maternal instincts. Perhaps if policies promoted secure attachment by allowing longer parental leave, the importance of the early moments and months would gain universal respect.

In the first three years, encouraging dependency is an emotional investment in future independence and health. But when mothers miss this chance early on, many find themselves bewildered when their previously compliant two-year-old becomes an angry, withdrawn adolescent. Little ones who learn to rely on themselves for comfort and safety become guarded teenagers who are hard to reach.

Alpha

Gordon Neufeld, Ph.D., a Vancouver-based clinical psychologist and co-author of the book *Hold On to Your Kids,* encourages women to access their inner "alpha" when they become mothers.[19] He describes an alpha mother as a woman who knows her strength and primacy in her baby's world. An alpha mother claims her place as her child's protector.

Neufeld asserts that anyone can provide this fierce care because vulnerable babies are so compelling and elicit our desire to protect them. While this is an interesting point, it oversimplifies a complex issue. Some mothers may easily step into the protective maternal role, but just as often, the intergenerational legacy of adversity, fear, and submission cripples a woman's protective instincts, overriding her conscious capacity to keep herself or her baby safe. She isn't purposefully causing harm, but toxic stress damages the neurocircuitry for maternal behaviors. "In fact, mothers who suffer from postpartum depression have very high cortisol levels in response to their baby's cries, which is like a PTSD response."[20]

In other words, protection seems natural, but regardless of how cute or compelling a baby might be, many frightened women simply don't have the internal resources for protection. Some compensate with overprotective measures, while others are underprotective. Either way, without healthy maternal protection, a daughter may grow up missing a felt sense of safety.

Allomothers

To protect vulnerable babies in the first three years, mothers may need to rely on caregivers known as *allomothers*. An allomother may be biologically related or not, but is emotionally invested in the well-being of the child. Fathers, grandparents, sisters, aunts, and nannies can be allomothers. Historically, allomothers helped the biological mother not because she was away, but because they were invested in her well-being and her infant's. Allomothers held and played with the baby while mom took a bath, got something to eat, or helped out other children.

In our fast-paced modern world, an allomother may not be a family member. She or he might be a nanny. For an allomother to successfully take over maternal tasks, he or she earns a place in the family.

If an allomother is spending more time with the little one than mom, the role of "favorite" might transfer in service of attachment processes. Secure attachment forms inside daily interactions with the primary caregiver, mother or allomother. Naturally, a mother may experience feelings of sadness as she surrenders her child to an alternate care-giver, but the loss is in service of the health and well-being of her little one, who deserves a secure base. In this way, maternal sacrifice *is* protective.

This is particularly true when working outside the home is essential. Some studies show that financial stress can negatively impact mothering, so when a mother works to ease financial burdens, the overall result can positively impact her children—especially with support from a reli-able allomother. However, Komisar explains that children of "two-parent working middle-class and upper-middle class families do less well in terms of their mental health when both parents work. . . . They feel their parent's detachment and interpret it as rejection."[21]

If an allomother isn't an option and a mother must rely on daycare when she is away for long periods of time, she may need to spend more time settling an anxious baby or child who has missed her all day. Protective mothers help their little ones with separation anxiety by making up for lost togetherness in nourishing ways. Putting away phones and playing right when getting home helps reestablish con-nection and trust after hours of being apart.

One of the most powerful protective measures to coun-teract lengthy hours apart is shared sleep. Physical proxim-ity at night promotes sensory connectedness, allowing sleep hours to fortify the baby's immature immune system and developing neurological health. I realize that nighttime sleep is a controversial issue, which is unfortunate. Sleep time shouldn't be stressful for little ones. Like mealtimes, it's a chance for connection and warmth and safety. Shar-ing nighttime hours fortifies the attachment process and will serve the little one as she matures. In this way, a shared sleep space is maternal protection in action. (For more information, see the Nighttime Parenting section on page 50 in Chapter 3.)

Protecting Growing Girls

As little girls grow, their needs for external protection do too. Just like adults, girls do better at work or play when someone has their back. Girls need a safe haven to return to after a day at school or time with friends—a place where they can make mistakes without punishment, learn boundaries without fear, and relax from the external pressures of growing up. Daughters do best when mothers create a secure environment with age-appropriate boundaries. With maternal protection, girls can tolerate a variety of stressors that come their way.

A mother's job as protector requires superpowers as her daughter grows and moves into mainstream culture. The world seems determined to steal her innocence. Sexual messages that exploit and objectify her flood the media and enter the privacy of our homes. In 1994, Mary Pipher's book *Reviving Ophelia* took the world by storm, enlightening parents about the risks facing their daughters. Over two decades later, new authors are still writing the same things about girls and stress. In spite of our efforts to empower girls and help them navigate our world, not much has changed. In *Under Pressure*, Lisa Damour, Ph.D., takes a close look at the rising number of girls who struggle with anxiety and mood problems. The number of girls who feel "nervous, worried, or fearful" jumped by 55 percent from 2009 to 2014, and the percentage of girls experiencing depression rose from 13 percent to 17 percent.[22] According to Damour's research, this increase is not because we are better at detecting these problems than we used to be—it's because we are seeing something new. The digital world has added new stress and anxiety for girls and their mothers.

When girls lack maternal protection, their adaptations to fear become more noticeable as they reach school age. Ongoing fear creates symptoms of traumatic stress. Jamie Howard, clinical psychologist at the Anxiety Disorder Center at the Child Mind Institute in New York City, encourages teachers to look for signs of trauma in their students. She states: "Kids that may seem like they have ADHD because they're really spacey may actually be distracted by trauma that's happened. And then kids who are avoidant of certain things or who have an exaggerated startle response might look oppositional."[23] Often, unprotected children appear overly energetic or day-dreamy (dissociated) while they are at school or daycare. Hyperactivity or being tuned out is simply a way of regulating a frightened brain. Signs of missing maternal protection may look like:

- Learning difficulties or concentration problems
- Spacing out
- Anxiety and excessive need to please
- Perfectionism
- Coordination problems and compromised posture
- Bursts of rage or tears
- Stomachaches, digestive issues, and headaches

A brain and body accustomed to distress is more easily triggered by things that happen during or after a long day at school. Emotional outbursts are common for all children trying to regulate their developing nervous systems, but for a child already stressed, fatigue or hunger can quickly escalate to rage or despair. Researchers call this phenomenon *kindling.*[24] Kindling explains how a child or adult can seem fine one minute and outraged or fearful the next. She is highly sensitive because her nervous system is on alert.

As little girls approach adolescence, personality adaptations may turn into mood disturbances that include eating problems, difficulty sleeping, and painful menstruation.

Girls and Sex

Misogyny explains self-hate and body hate. The sexual alarm system explains sexual fear. Mix these two powerful forces together and we have a potent cocktail that damages sexual development for women. I've been writing about female sexuality for well over a decade, and I am saddened by how little has changed in those years. Although girls have more opportunity for independence, they still struggle with feeling safe, with body image, and with relationships. Sex education hasn't changed much, except for the unfortunate reality that porn, as we know, is a new teacher.[25] On the "digital street corner," girls are learning that danger and sex go together. That strangulation is part of foreplay. That being hot is everything.

Hotness as a virtue shows up when female role models demonstrate sexual "empowerment" by crotch grabbing, pole dancing, and gestures that seem to exhibit dominance rather than freedom. In Peggy Orenstein's excellent book *Girls and Sex*, she draws on interviews with adolescents to take a look at the modern sexual forces facing our daughters. Orenstein explores the contradiction for girls who have more opportunities and education but still deal with dehumanizing sexual pressures. She shares a comment from an interview with one girl who says, "Usually the opposite of a negative is a positive, but when you're talking about girls and sex, the opposite of 'slut' is 'prude,' both of which are negative. So what are you supposed to do?"[26]

Orenstein explores the same sexual double bind that I wrote about in my book *Ready to Heal*. A double bind is an impossible situation where all the choices lead to negative outcomes. I found four distinct beliefs that emerge for women from this double bind:

- If I am sexual, I am bad.

- I must be good to be worthy of love.

- I am not really a woman unless someone desires me sexually or romantically.

- I must be sexual to be lovable.

These beliefs teach us that to be loved we must be sexy. But if we're *too* sexy, we're bad. Only good girls are lovable, but if you want love, you must be sexually desirable. These four beliefs create a psychological impasse that freezes healthy sexual development and sets the stage for love and sex to become painful or addictive habits rather than expressions of joy and pleasure. In fact, as Orenstein eloquently explains in her TED talk, girls don't generally consider their own sexual pleasure as a priority. If the partner has an orgasm, that is good enough. Despite progress for girls in some areas, sexist double standards seem to stick with us, for both mothers and daughters.

Protection and Female Sexuality

Mothers often land on extreme ends of the sexual protection spectrum: either overprotective or underprotective. Overprotective mothers teach their daughters to be afraid of boys and sex. Abstinence and avoidance are their protection strategies. Underprotective mothers turn the other way when their daughters need help. Underprotective mothers don't set curfews or limit exposure to technology. They may sacrifice their daughters to fathers, brothers, and uncles. What is the balance? What is the recipe for raising sexually healthy girls? I'm not sure there is one.

The same patriarchal culture that poisons female sexual development trains us to defer to authority for educating our daughters. Mothers hope churches or schools can teach daughters about sex and safety, but this form of educating isn't going well. "The way we educate young people about sexuality is not working. We expect them to dismiss their instinctive desires and curiosities even as we bombard them with images that imply that lust is the most important appetite and hotness the most impressive virtue," writes Ariel Levy.[27]

When men become fathers, their unexamined beliefs about women, gender, and sexuality may not help. In overt and covert ways, fathers may perpetuate female objectification and victimization. Sometimes their own lust leaks out as a daughter enters puberty and her body changes. Fathers may comment on these changes in ways that leave a daughter feeling icky or confused. Fathers who fail to protect their daughters might demonstrate inappropriate behaviors like commenting on the appearance of a waitress or comparing a daughter's body to her mother's body, teaching by example that women are objects.

In a recent research experiment, a mom spent seven days online pretending to be an 11-year-old girl. She uploaded a generic photo with a caption reading, "v excited to see my friends this weekend at carly's party! Ilysm!!" Within minutes after posting the material, this pseudo 11-year-old had 7 video calls, text-chats with 17 men, and seen the genitals of 11 of those men.[28] Sloane Ryan, who runs the special projects team at Bark, a tech company committed to child safety, reports that in 2018, Bark alerted the FBI to 99 child predators, and in 2019, the number is more than 300 and growing. Ryan illustrates how predators talk:

You're so pretty.
You should be a model.
I'm older than you.
What would you do if you were here, baby?
Would you [sex act] if you were here?
Have you seen one before, baby?

Baby, you're so beautiful.
Talk to me, baby.
I want you to [sex act], baby.
Just get on video chat, baby.
Don't be shy, baby.[29]

To put it very simply, unprotected access to the open Internet isn't safe for children. While Internet access offers learning opportunities, it's also an added burden for mothers who strive to protect their daughters from predators and harmful sexual material. It's a fast-growing monster. When I work with parents who are overwhelmed with this issue, I keep it simple. Think of unmonitored Internet as cocaine. While this might sound extreme, it gets the point across: the Internet is addictive and dangerous. Kids need supervision and limits with electronic devices.

Siblings and Protection

When daughters who are still little girls are put in a position to care for their siblings, they find themselves face-to-face with adult responsibilities they aren't ready for and didn't choose. When Janet was a little girl, her mother was very ill. It was Janet's job to care for her older brother and father. She was only six when she learned to make the beds, prepare meals (mostly tuna sandwiches), and clean the house. As an adult, Janet hates to cook and can't stand the smell of tuna. She rarely leaves her house. Janet's story might seem extreme, but it's not uncommon for a mother to use her daughter as a babysitter or a housekeeper. While helping out the family can create a sense of belonging for a daughter, when the job is too much and too lonely, caretaking becomes frightening. The responsibility is too big.

Furthermore, when a child is burdened with too much of her mother's work, siblings are robbed of the chance to be siblings. One becomes the caretaker, carrying the load of responsibility, while the younger siblings feel controlled, jealous, or victimized. My client Rose was an only child until her parents divorced and her mother started dating a musician who had a baby. Rose was nine years old when she found herself in charge of a little stepsister. Her mother was distracted with new friends and nightly events. She left Rose alone with the baby a lot. Rose was overwhelmed by the responsibility and the lonely nights at home without her mother. "Sometimes the baby would cry and cry and nothing seemed to help. I called my mom, but she just told me to let her cry. It was so awful . . . listening to that little baby cry."

Understandably, Rose grew up tired, resentful, and worried that she didn't like babies or children. She delayed having a family, convinced that she would be a terrible mother. After a few years of treatment, however, she changed her mind. Healing the pain of maternal neglect helped her reclaim her lost youth and make a more conscious decision about motherhood.

The Mother Hunger Spectrum

The adversity children face doesn't have to be severe to create deep physiological and psychological changes that can lead to Mother Hunger. The severity of Mother Hunger is unique to each daughter, and the intensity of adaptations depends on the degree of missing maternal protection and the availability of alternate safe adults.

In adolescence and adulthood, adaptations might look like constant low-grade depression or chronic anxiety. Attention problems, hyperactivity, and perfectionism are also evidence of Mother Hunger. So are addictive habits—addictions are a form of self-soothing and a resourceful way to avoid pain.

If you didn't have adequate maternal protection, hopefully the anxiety and stress you live with makes more sense now. Protecting yourself for so many years takes a toll. Living with fear and anxiety wears down your immune system, leaving you vulnerable to physical symptoms like migraines, joint pain, bowel disorders, painful PMS, or autoimmune problems. You might be attracted to powerful people who are manipulative and perhaps dangerous. You might have addictions or compulsions.

Some things are just too hard to know until change is actually possible. Understanding how your symptoms are related to missing maternal protection may reduce your shame. Healing flows more easily without the added burden of shame, which is why if you struggle with addiction, addressing addictive behaviors is a powerful step in the right direction. Addiction always leads to shame, and shame interferes with the legitimate hurt that needs your care.

Many of you are tired. You have been trying to protect yourself for years, and you're drained from working too much or too hard, from overeating and undereating, or from loving in destructive ways.

Addiction may begin as a way to appease a mother and adapt to her vulnerability. The addictive behavior begins with the innocent hope that *If I can simply do the right thing (say the right thing, be the right thing), she will protect and love me. I can calm down.* Dr. Gabor Maté states, "At the core of every addiction is an emptiness based in abject fear."[30] Addiction is an attempt to regulate fear and despair—fear of being unlovable or alone, fear that grows without a fundamental sense of safety.

Here are some common examples:

- **Love addiction**: Earning maternal love unconsciously with romantic partners. Love addiction may include an insatiable craving for physical touch. Sometimes this can lead to a sexual addiction.

- **Eating patterns**: Earning a mother's approval by looking a certain way that required food restriction. Sometimes overeating is a way to show anger toward a controlling mother.

- **Working too much**: Compulsive busyness might have gained a mother's approval as a child. As an adult, it might offer you the feeling of safety and control you craved as a child.

- **Exercising too much**: Working out to the point of injury and yet being unable to rest is a sign of feeling unsafe.

Do any of these addictive tendencies resonate for you?

Uncovering Fear

- Recall a time you felt safe as a little girl. What was happening? Who was there?

- How do you re-create the sensation of safety in your current life?

- Recall a frightening moment from your past. What was happening? Who was there? Where was your mother?

- Do you re-create fear in your current life?

Anxiety Rescue

When anxiety gets intense, try this quick age-old intervention. Alternate nostril breathing, which is part of some hatha yoga practices, is a very helpful exercise when you wake up feeling anxious or have difficulty falling asleep. You can even use it when you're stuck in traffic.

Alternate nostril breathing helps relax your body and mind, reduces nervous system activity, and brings an overall sense of well-being. "Science suggests that you stimulate both sides of the brain and ancient wisdom believes that you gain energetic balance in alternate nostril breathing."[31]

To start, close one nostril and breathe in through the other to the count of five. Close both nostrils for the count of five. Then exhale from the other nostril to the count of five. Repeat for a few rounds until you feel relief.

Practicing alternate nostril breathing can intervene in a panic attack and may also help you become more focused and aware. If you enjoy the effects of breathing this way, regular practice may help you become more mindful and enhance your healing.

Replacing Maternal Protection

Dreams are windows into the soul, and without fail, women who suffer a lack of maternal protection have nightmarish sleep patterns and dreams. In my years of clinical practice, I've noticed a theme to these dreams. Women who didn't feel safe as little girls dream of homes that are flooding, burning, or infested with rodents. Inside the house, they are trapped and alone. There is no comfort. As treatment progresses, however, these dreams change. I know healing is happening when the rodents are gone; when hallways lead to magical rooms that weren't there before; when, outside, flowers are growing. The home, which is a metaphor for the body, is blooming.

From years of practice, I am confident that you can begin healing your brain with visualization and mindful intention. Start when you are comfortable and somewhere safe, maybe right before going to sleep at night. Close your eyes. Picture the home that you see when you dream at night. How does it feel to be inside? What does it look like? What do you need inside this home and outside this home to feel safe and cozy?

Open your eyes. Now take a look at pictures of beautiful homes in print magazines or on the Internet. Focus on images that make your heart happy. When you feel your spirit lift, bask in the sensation. Beauty is good for your brain. You are building a dream home that will become your safe place—a place that will soothe the fear that's been with you for so long. Take your time. Get creative with this exercise by bookmarking images or posting them around your space. You are curating an inner sanctuary where there is no threat.

When you prepare for sleep each night, wander through these images in your mind. Close your eyes, cover yourself in a heavy blanket, and let your mind imagine what it will be like to live in this place you have designed. This conscious nightly ritual directly influences your inner home. As the landscape of your mind improves, so will the quality of your sleep and mood throughout the following day.

CHAPTER 7

GUIDANCE

A daughter watches her mother for clues about how to be a woman. She studies her mother's friends, her mother's style, her mother's mannerisms, and the relationships her mother has with men. In this way, a mother is a guide. A mother raising a daughter is never really off-duty. She guides by example, teaching her daughter to be gentle and strong, to love others without giving herself away, and to care for her female body. A mother who knows how to rest and care for herself teaches her daughter that she is worthwhile and important.

Misguided Mothers

Before we discuss healthy maternal guidance, it's important to acknowledge the years of damaging *misguidance* women have been given about mothering. Depending on the decade, mothers learned that formula was the best nutrition for their baby and the cry-it-out method was the way to teach independence. Generations of well-meaning mothers have learned to ignore their own instincts, deferring to the "experts" as they navigate the emotions that come with motherhood. Becoming a mother is a transition like no other, and it's tragic that the medical community and child development experts don't have current information about early attachment needs. For this reason, many mothers need better guidance to make important choices about their infants and toddlers.

Frequently, mothers seek psychotherapy when their daughters start to have problems, often right around the middle school years. During these challenging times, mothers may quit working or try other ways to become involved with their teenage daughters who are in crisis. Naturally, they want to guide their girls. Over and over, I hear their disappointment and surprise when things don't go well. Comments like "She doesn't listen to me" or "She's always angry at me" fill the therapy room as they wonder where their sweet little girls have gone.

For maternal guidance to be effective, there must first be a trusted bond. For daughters who missed out on early maternal nurturance or protection, the important role of maternal guidance is compromised. Daughters who learn from an early age to "suck up" separation anxieties or defend themselves have been going it alone for a long time. Many have a hard time when a mother suddenly wants to be more involved. Conflict is natural in this scenario: A mother wants to help but feels unappreciated when her efforts aren't well received. A daughter gets angry when her mother can't see how grown up she is. Mothers may demand respect with fear-inducing or controlling behaviors. This is not maternal guidance. Control teaches compliance. Compliant daughters are at risk for becoming vulnerable women without healthy boundaries or self-awareness because they learned to appease their mothers.

When Maternal Guidance Is Harmful

Maternal guidance is a sacrifice of time, wisdom, and energy with no guarantee that a daughter will appreciate the effort. In fact, mothers who look for gratitude or affirmation from their daughters place an unnecessary burden on girls as they develop a sense of who they are. Adrienne Brodeur's memoir, *Wild Game*, has been a sort of literary phenomenon—a memoir that captured national attention for its gorgeously written prose and for the complicated emotional betrayal the author reveals. For us, it serves as a terrific real-life example of how lack of healthy maternal guidance can arrest a daughter's emotional development and damage her sexual innocence.

The story begins the summer of Adrienne's 14th year. It begins with a romance—not the story one might anticipate from a blossoming young woman, but a drama where actors are assigned the wrong parts. Adrienne is not the romantic lead. Rather, that part goes to her boundaryless mother, Malabar. With insatiable force, Malabar steals the show while her adoring understudy shadows every move.

Through Adrienne's watchful eyes, we have a front-row seat to Malabar's love affair with her husband's best friend, Ben. We witness Malabar act like a teenager as her infatuation with Ben takes over. Like most of us when we fall in love, Malabar wants a witness. Someone to share the excitement with. Unfortunately, rather than turning to an age-appropriate friend, or perhaps even a therapist, Malabar takes advantage of her daughter, waking her in the middle of the night to proclaim her feelings for Ben. Sounding more like a schoolgirl than a mother, she pleads, "Aren't you happy for me, Rennie?" Thrilled to be taken into her mother's confidence, we follow Adrienne's gaze. "I looked at her face and into her eyes, dark and dewy with hope, and all at once, I was happy for her. And for me. Malabar was falling in love, and she'd picked me as her confidante, a role I hadn't realized I longed for until that moment."[1] And just like that, our willing, vulnerable narrator finds herself in a love triangle.

Malabar's insatiable lust for romantic distraction devours her daughter's free time as she involves her in the clandestine affair. By sharing each detail and using her daughter as a friend, Malabar creates a dynamic where Adrienne feels that "the 'we' had always been my mother and me" instead of Malabar and Ben.[2]

Through the wordless mirroring process, daughters are wired to learn from mothers. Ideally, for this learning to feel good, we want to admire our mother—to be inspired by her. We see Adrienne's longing to be proud of her mother as she tries to justify Malabar's affair in her mind.

> Perhaps this could be a good thing. . . . Perhaps in the fall, when school started, my mother would get dressed for carpool. No more coat over her nightgown or sheet marks on her puffy morning face. Maybe she'd brush her hair, smear some gloss across her lips, and greet the children on our route with a cheery "Hello" like all of the other mothers.[3]

Mothers who use their daughters for friendship not only misuse their power—they avoid growing up. They take a shortcut to adulthood. Rather than face their own insecurities and risk bonding with adult women (who might judge or reject them), these mothers bask in the easy proximity, vulnerability, and admiration of their daughters.

Movies and literature often romanticize the idea of mother and daughter as best friends. To tell a story, Hollywood gives children adult-like personality traits. Terms like *mini me* or *bestie* in reference to a daughter hide the important role of a maternal guide. But the idea that mom and daughter could be best friends ignores the power imbalance between them. A daughter loves her mother but needs her differently than a friend. She needs her mother's nurturance, protection, and guidance—a job description way beyond friendship.

Enmeshment

Adrienne shares a resounding truth for many women when she explains to the reader that her mother was "the most central and important person in my life, even if I wished it were otherwise."[4] In the privacy of stolen moments, Malabar misuses her daughter's adoration. *Wild Game* is a spectacular display of an insidious type of emotional abuse known as *enmeshment*.

Enmeshment is what happens when a parent manipulates a child to meet his or her own needs. Salvador Minuchin, an Argentinian family therapist who developed structural family therapy, first named the concept of enmeshment to describe family systems where adult children adhere to their parent's interests or beliefs at the expense of their own.[5] Dr. Ken Adams further adapts the concept of enmeshment as covert or emotional incest in his book *Silently Seduced*. Covert incest happens when an enmeshing parent treats a child as a partner. In this way, a psychological marriage forms between parent and child, where the child feels undue loyalty to her parent.[6] Daughters rarely identify parental enmeshment as harmful, because it feels good to be singled out. Being chosen as the favorite seems like a privilege. But the cost is high. When a mother's care is too intense, an enmeshed daughter caters to her mother's moods, needs, and desires while losing the chance to know her own.

If enmeshment describes your upbringing, I want you to know that it's normal to feel used and resentful. You are tired. You may feel like you have already been married, so you avoid intimate relationships. Unconsciously, committing to someone feels like betraying Mom, or frankly, it's just too exhausting. If you do commit, it's common to pick uninspiring partners—in this way, you keep the primary bond with Mom intact. Herein is a loss of choice. Your body is making decisions for you without your cognitive awareness. As you recognize the legacy of enmeshment, you can move away from the duty of being your mother's source and reclaim your own authority.

Mirroring

Each daughter is wired to mirror her mother, absorbing her mother's thoughts, emotions, and dreams into herself. "A connection with someone they experience as wise and good creates possibilities for them to experience themselves as good too."[7] But some mothers don't have the tools for loving guidance. When a mother behaves in troublesome ways (like conducting an affair, sharing the details with her daughter, and manipulating her into participating), a daughter's psyche mirrors the experience. Such mirroring creates guilt and shame that doesn't belong to her.

Wild Game paints a vivid picture of harmful mirroring as we watch Malabar lay a legacy of guilt and shame on her daughter's back. With no regard for Adrienne's well-being, Malabar steals her daughter's innocence and stains her with infidelity.

Infidelity and the lying that go along with it generally make a person feel guilty. But not in Malabar's case. She never seems disturbed or embarrassed by her sexual behaviors or parenting choices. She shows no remorse for stealing her daughter's time away from college. Nor is she apologetic for involving Adrienne in a massive cover-up for her affair.

When a person behaves in shameless ways, disowned shame often attaches to someone else. Michelle Mays, founder and clinical director for the Center for Relational Recovery in Leesburg, Virginia, explains this dynamic beautifully: "When someone is behaving in an offensive or violating manner, the healthy shame they are not connected to . . . spills over onto the offended party (the betrayed partner) who then ends up carrying the shame of what happened." In therapeutic circles, we call this psychological phenomenon *carried shame*.

Carried Shame

In *Wild Game*, Malabar has multiple victims who could carry her shame, but Adrienne is the youngest and most vulnerable. The central crime in this story is less about marital infidelity than the theft of our narrator's childhood. Adrienne is the true betrayed partner, much more than Malabar's husband, Charles. We see Adrienne struggle with guilt and shame that doesn't belong to her. "Whenever my mother was away—purportedly rescuing Julia but in reality staying in a hotel room with her husband's best friend—it was my job to look after Charles."[8]

Although Adrienne describes taking care of her stepfather as "not difficult," it was an emotional burden that didn't belong to her. Malabar put her in an impossible psychological bind.

> The only hard part of taking care of Charles was the lying. . . . At first, it felt simple. But over

time . . . it became a heavy weight. When you lie to someone you love—and I did love Charles—let alone when you lie so often that the lie seems truer than the actual truth, you lose the only thing that matters: the possibility of real connection. I lost the ability to connect with Charles the day the first lie fell from my lips. Over time, I began to lose it with myself too.[9]

We can see Adrienne's struggle. It's as if she's the one cheating instead of her mother. Adrienne carries her mother's shame and, in the process, loses her innocence.

Malabar's egregious misguidance intensifies as she faces the possibility of discovery and comes unglued. Calling Adrienne, who is away for college, she exclaims, "Ben is everything to me. Absolutely everything. My life isn't worth living if I lose him."[10] The emotional enmeshment escalates to a crisis as Malabar shamelessly shares her innermost thoughts, illuminating for Adrienne her lack of value in her mother's eyes. "If Ben was everything to my mother, then what was I? Was I not worth living for too?" Yet, on the other hand, her love and loyalty belong to Malabar. She's afraid for her mother's life. She has no choice. In a Malabar trance, Adrienne gathers her precious energy, abandons her college studies, and rescues her relentless mother.

In *Wild Game*, maternal guidance is heartbreaking as we see Malabar misguide Adrienne. Her lessons include seduction, secrets, and manipulations. If your mother put you in the role of her friend, you may have an unconscious belief that it is your job to make her happy or affirm her mothering, or that it's up to you to give her life meaning. You may struggle with ambivalence, feeling guilty for wanting your own space.

Femininity Training
and Maternal Guidance

Maternal guidance gets little cultural respect, so many well-meaning mothers are confused about modeling feminine strength for their daughters.

Femininity training, or learning the "girl code," impacts not only the work that women do but also how women are supposed to behave in relationship to men. The girl code teaches women to serve, seduce, and submit to men while competing with one another for male attention. Mothers who have awareness of these cultural messages try to minimize the impact of the girl code on their daughters. By monitoring media exposure, sharing domestic labor with their partner and sons, and celebrating a daughter's achievements and talents, wise mothers do their best to mitigate harmful femininity training. But generations of maternal inheritance may pass the girl code between mothers and daughters in spite of amazing effort, quietly infecting the guidance women provide. Compromised maternal guidance shows up in myriad ways, some of which include:

- Competing with daughters
  for a partner's attention
- Carrying the weight of household
  duties with resentment
- Showing a preference for sons over daughters
- Escaping reality with addictive and
  secretive behaviors

Understandably, mothers may quietly grieve the loss of their own youth and beauty as they witness their daughters becoming young women. But daughters lose a trustworthy guide when mothers mismanage this rite of passage and steal joy from their blooming girls by competing with them. In the process, mothers sometimes teach their daughters that women can't be trusted.

Cultural Influence as Guidance

Without healthy maternal guidance, daughters are at the mercy of cultural influences that construct femininity. Being female is biology, but "femininity" is a social and cultural creation based on multiple systemic factors. For generations, women learned that worth comes from being nice and attractive. And while education and career options expand, displays of anger in the workplace are reserved for men. The media is part of femininity training as the "male gaze" uses the female body for marketing and entertainment. Marissa Korbel, editor of the Rumpus, does a remarkable job explaining how women are impacted by femininity training as she describes her own:

> On one hand, [culture was telling me] I had agency, autonomy, and responsibility for my body, my choices, my life. On the other, [the larger culture was teaching me that] I didn't really know what was best for me. I couldn't be trusted to say what things were. My mother knew better. My father. My teachers. My elders in general. And then, when it came to my desire, men knew, or were supposed to know, better than I did. Except the bad ones. If only it were easier to know which ones were bad.[11]

Cultural programming impacts mothers and daughters, complicating maternal guidance when it comes to sexuality. As understudy to our mother, we form an internal compass that directs our desires and feelings about our body by watching her. Many of us feel confused as our body develops and we first feel sexual desire. Caught in a sexual and social double bind that asks us to be good (saintly, pure, and sacrificial) and bad (sexy, erotic, and seductive) at the same time, we aren't sure how to navigate erotic feelings in a healthy manner. When our mother hasn't made peace with this double bind herself, we are on our own to find other guides.

Fathers and Daughters

When it comes to guidance, daughters benefit if and when their fathers are involved. Research shows that fathers who value relationships are more likely to have securely attached children. A father's primary job is to protect and support the mother so she can build a base for her daughter in the early months and years. Once this base is secure, however, fathers get more time on stage. Research illustrates how a father's play sensitivity seems to be a critical part of the attachment process with his child in the same way that maternal caregiving sensitivity is.[12] Play is the language of paternal love and guidance.

Paternal guidance in the form of praise, helpful limits, and shared time increases a daughter's confidence. Studies show that if a father enjoys his daughter and encourages her natural strengths, she may be more inclined to see herself as capable. Research suggests that daughters whose fathers who are involved with homework and encourage their daughters to take challenging courses have higher levels of sociability, a higher level of school performance, and fewer behavior problems. Interestingly, daughters of fathers like these are also more likely to have high-paying jobs as adults.[13]

Unfortunately, misguided parents sometimes compete for their daughter's love and devotion. They miss the important truth: each parent is necessary and has a unique purpose. They can't both be the "favorite" all the time. It's helpful when parents take turns being a primary guide. Daughters love their parents or caregivers unconditionally and want them to be happy. But when parents are uncertain of their purpose and look to the daughter to choose one of them over the other, that's unfair. If your parents put you in a position to choose sides, it's very likely that you are living with a haunting sadness from being put in the middle of their insecurities. Part of your healing is letting go of this emotional burden that was never yours to carry.

Paternal Sexual Guidance

Daughters learn about sex from both parents. Growing up, a daughter watches how her father treats her mother to learn how men behave with women. When a father takes time away from his hobbies and work to spend time with Mom, a daughter observes that Mom is a priority to him. When a mother and father enjoy each other, play together, and show affection with one another, a daughter has a powerful buffer from the dominant cultural lessons outside the home.

But parents are products of our culture and the ideology that permeates our sexual landscape, as we discussed in Chapter 5. As such, it's not uncommon for daughters to see their fathers judging and commenting on the way women look. Fathers who are unaware of their impact and responsibility for sexual guidance may bring "locker room talk" to the dinner table or flirt with waitresses in a restaurant. Girls learn from such fathers that feminine power comes with sex appeal, that being sexy gets attention. Overt signs of sexual double standards like these teach a daughter how to behave, perpetuating the dominant culture's sexual messages.

Guiding girls toward healthy sexuality seems like an impossible task in a world where pornography is available with such ease and privacy—and is not necessarily seen as problematic. A colleague recently shared with me how her client exclaimed, "I've been watching porn since I was 12 . . . now I finally get to be in it!" A client of mine, Maria, who has a Ph.D. and a busy career, told me that the most power she ever felt was when she traded sex for money in her early 20s. "He would never admit it, but if my father could have seen me work, he would have been proud." Maria's sense of how her father might feel about her sex work may or may not be accurate, but the message is clear: sex, men, and power are linked.

Sexual Shame

All women in a patriarchal culture are highly suscepti- ble to sexual shame, but the legacy of harmful sexual mes- sages may be intensified for marginalized groups of women. Women of color and lesbian women, who don't fit into white heterosexist norms, become targets for unwanted sexual attention in media and movies. Lesbian women are often forced to actively face their sexuality in ways that heterosex- ual women are not.[14] For a lesbian, the issue of maternal guid- ance is layered with complexity as she looks to her mother to understand herself. Mothers and daughters have enough difficulty navigating the topic of sex, but add homophobia to the mix and it's a recipe for Mother Hunger to fester and pollute a daughter's core self. When sexual identity threat- ens belonging, daughters understandably may withhold the truth from their mothers to avoid possible rejection. Daugh- ters who can't turn to their mothers to talk about sex and ask questions, for whatever reason, may maintain a secret life, which is not only lonely but also a breeding ground for addictions and other harmful behaviors.

Mother Hunger and Loss of Maternal Guidance

As a daughter, you may have missed out on the guidance you needed from your mother.

Maybe you learned that it wasn't safe to be different— you may have picked up on your mother's hidden hope that you would be just like her. To avoid criticism, you learned to fold the laundry like she did, fix your hair the way she wanted, and stay out of her way when she was stressed. You learned to keep your opinions to yourself if they were different from hers.

Or perhaps your mother needed you to rise above her and become something better. You had to be *amazing* so she could feel better about herself. She had little patience with your natural mistakes, because your behavior reflected her mothering ability. Her unlived life was yours to fulfill.

If you identify with having had poor maternal guidance, you may often feel anxiety, because your behavior and achievements don't reflect your true desires. Perhaps your life feels like your mother's résumé builder instead of your own journey. Life without maternal guidance can lead to a few of the following characteristics:

- Excessive caretaking in relationships

- Deep insecurity

- Difficulty making decisions that reflect your own desires

- Chronic guilt and a belief that you're never enough (for your mother)

- Constantly comparing yourself to other girls and women

- Dissatisfaction with your body image and appearance

- Loyalty to abusive people, usually your mother or people like her

- Overinvolvement with your own children, with periodic abandonment to take care of your mother instead

Without healthy maternal guidance, it's difficult to fully integrate and know your value and worth. Dr. Christiane Northrup writes, "Our culture gives girls the [false] message that their bodies, their lives, and their femaleness demand an apology."[15] This makes belonging a challenge.

More than anything, we want to belong and be included among other women. But along the way, we may discover that belonging means hiding our strength. To fit in, we play small. In a culture that devalues qualities such as empathy, collaboration, and connection, owning our attributes can feel like a liability.

Part of the hurt and longing of Mother Hunger is the search for your mother's power. Healing means you claim your own power in ways that feel healthy and constructive. Becoming the authority for your life may require you to find new guides and role models—people who inspire you. Healing Mother Hunger brings you the opportunity to rebuild damaged dreams and goals—and to no longer apologize for being a woman.

Finding Guidance

- What is good about being a woman?

- What is difficult about being a woman?

- When did another woman stand up for me? How did it feel?

- When did I last stand up for or support another woman?

- What are women really like?

- Did you admire your mother?

- Did your mother have friendships with other women? Were they happy relationships?

- What did you learn about sex from your mother and other caregivers?

- Is there a woman you admire, who you can trust, in your life?

Based on the answers to the questions above, you can identify where you need guidance. Guidance requires a role model. Who in your life seems to have solved the issue you're facing? How does she treat her friends? Do other women like her?

When you find a role model, spend time with this woman. If she is someone on TV or in a movie, imagine what she might do. Replacing maternal guidance is your chance to choose women you admire and learn from them.

CHAPTER 8

THIRD-DEGREE
MOTHER HUNGER

After a few years of working closely with women suffering from Mother Hunger, I recognized a diverse spectrum for this injury. While Mother Hunger is universally unpleasant for everyone, some forms of Mother Hunger are worse than others. Warning: This chapter uncovers what happens when daughters experience maternal cruelty. If this is not your story, you might want to skip this section. If you survived an abusive mother, this chapter is for you. It will validate your despair, but it will also be hard to read. Healing—identifying, understanding, and remembering—can be as painful as the original abuse.

Judy and Édith

Third-Degree Mother Hunger came to life on the big screen in two award-winning performances of iconic women who brought song into our hearts: Renée Zellweger as Judy Garland in the 2019 Oscar-winning *Judy* and Marion Cotillard as Édith Piaf in 2007 in *La Vie en Rose*. Both incredible movies vividly depict two girls who experienced maternal cruelty and abandonment in the first 24 months of life. Born to women who didn't want them, who couldn't care for them, they each suffered immensely as they made their way in life. Tragically, and with an eerie similarity, they both died very young.

Judy Garland, the beloved Dorothy in *The Wizard of Oz*, died at age 47 from complications related to alcohol and drugs. Édith Piaf, sometimes referred to as the French Judy Garland, also died at age 47 from liver complications related to drugs and alcohol. In their short, troubled lives, both women struggled immeasurably as they married and divorced numerous times, made and lost money, and battled health problems, including addictions.

At age 11, Judy Garland "sang like a woman three times her age, with a broken heart."[1] Édith Piaf, beloved by the French people, also had a hauntingly mature voice as a child. Singing on the streets by age 7, she captured the hearts of passersby.[2]

Judy's parents were vaudeville entertainers who already had two daughters and did not want another baby. When they discovered a new pregnancy, they searched for someone to perform an abortion without success. Judy came into a cold, harsh world, void of nurturance and protection. She was rehearsing and performing with her sisters by the age of 3, and as early as age 10, her mother was supplying her with diet pills during the day and sedatives at night to keep her compliant. Judy shared a poignant story about her mother's guidance with Barbara Walters: "She'd say, 'You get out there and sing or I'll wrap you around the bedpost and break you off short!'"[3]

Like Judy, Édith was born to an entertainer—a street singer—who wasn't ready to be a mother. As a baby, Édith was left with her old and failing maternal grandmother. Édith nearly died from complications of meningitis and starvation. Eventually, a relative found her covered in lice and took her to live with her paternal grandmother, who ran a brothel. Although not a place we typically think of as suitable for a young girl, there she found the first comfort she had ever known. A young woman working as a prostitute took Édith under her wing and gave her affection and tenderness. But at the age 7, her first loving bond ended abruptly and tragically when her father came and took her away to tour and perform in the circus with him.

Without the shelter of maternal care, both girls were vulnerable to the men around them. Louis Mayer, the MGM studio director, had too much access to Judy's upbringing. He restricted her food, nicknamed her "my little hunchback" (making fun of her curved spine), and sexually molested her.[4] Similarly, Édith endured sexual violations from her biological father. Like Judy, Édith's posture was never quite right, as she also had a curved spine. She suffered frequent hunger and chronic neglect, and by the age of 17, she left her father and the circus to make her way, singing on the streets of Paris.[5]

In an interview, Judy Garland shared that the "only time I felt wanted when I was a kid was when I was on stage, performing" and referred to her mother as the "true Wicked Witch of the West."[6] Similarly, Édith Piaf thrived with audience feedback that gave her a sense of belonging. She bloomed when a nightclub owner discovered her and brought her onto a stage. At the age of 18, her career was just beginning, when she became pregnant and gave birth to a baby girl. Repeating her mother's love, she routinely abandoned her daughter for the stage, leaving mothering duties to her baby's father. Tragically, her daughter died from meningitis just before the age of 2.[7]

Similarly, Judy experienced early pregnancy. She had her first abortion at age 19 and a second before giving birth to her first daughter at 23. In the first of many suicide attempts, Judy slashed her throat when she was 28. Using a broken glass bottle, she enacted the epigenetic legacy of a mother who wanted to cut her baby from her body. She shared that she lost her self-confidence and all she wanted to do was eat and hide. Judy went on to have five unhappy marriages, the last one to a man 20 years younger.[8]

Édith Piaf's last husband, after many unhappy relationships, was also 20 years younger than she was.[9] Both women were dependent on drugs and alcohol throughout their lives, and despite the income that followed fame, they struggled with homelessness and debt. Both had nightmarish physical health problems that included hepatitis, exhaustion, kidney ailments, "nervous breakdowns," weight fluctuations, and multiple physical injuries.

As an adult, Judy grew so compromised that she missed performances, showed up late, or walked onto the stage fueled by drugs and alcohol. Adoring fans lost respect for her. On one occasion, she was booed off the stage while people threw food.[10] The only place she had ever felt loved became a nightmare. Like Judy, Édith's last performances were a desperate display of health problems and addiction. High on morphine and alcohol, she struggled to stand up and remember her songs. Despite a sad end, her death was mourned across France as thousands lined the route of her funeral procession.[11]

Complex Trauma

Like Judy Garland and Édith Piaf, women with extreme forms of Mother Hunger have symptoms of complex post-traumatic stress disorder. Complex post-traumatic stress disorder (CPTSD) differs from post-traumatic stress disorder (PTSD) because it is caused by repeated trauma. When little ones endure parental abuse, the incidents are rarely a singular event, and the childhood trauma is ongoing. The prolonged nature of this kind of adversity creates challenging, enduring symptoms that may not go away, because living with constant fear changes the brain during rapid growth periods. In Judith Herman's research on complex post-traumatic stress disorder, she documents adults receiving psychiatric treatment, noting that "survivors of childhood abuse display significantly more insomnia, sexual dysfunction, dissociation, anger, suicidality, self-mutilation, drug addiction, and alcoholism than other patients."[12]

If you grew up with a mother who was cruel and frightening, her behavior required your autonomic nervous system to stay in overdrive. Under constant threat, developing brain pathways meant for social behavior took a back seat to the pathways meant for safety. Unused neurons became weaker and less able to carry signals that govern attention and mood regulation. At the same time, pathways designed for self-preservation gained strength to keep you alert for signs of danger. Complex trauma explains why you were wound up, energetic, anxious, or irritable as a child and may still feel this way as an adult. Like someone anticipating a blow, your body and mind are wired for war.

When you understand that your nervous system has been shaped by early, ongoing fear, and that your body is doing its job to protect you, it can be very empowering. Reactions that might cause you to feel ashamed and different from others begin to make sense. You are not broken. Your body is simply biologically wired in protective mode and responds very quickly, below your awareness, to anything that is a reminder of childhood abuse. In other words, you don't "choose" a reaction that may be extreme or frightening to yourself and others. Your response is automatic and somatic (based in the body).

While brain neuroplasticity offers the possibility to change and heal these reactions, adults with CPTSD face a more rigorous healing process than those with milder forms of Mother Hunger. For this reason, I give extreme forms of Mother Hunger like these a separate name—a name that captures what it's like to survive the complete loss of maternal nurturance, protection, or guidance. A name to illuminate the barren landscape of chronic fear and isolation. A name for a painful relational burn. The legacy of maternal abuse is what I call *Third-Degree Mother Hunger.*

Third-Degree Mother Hunger shares symptoms with personality disorders like borderline personality disorder, bipolar disorder, and dissociative identity disorder. But I don't consider Third-Degree Mother Hunger a disorder; it's a profound attachment injury that creates a constellation of symptoms that make life unbearable.

Patterns of relationship instability—idealizing someone one moment but in the next experiencing the same person as cruel—are normal for those with Third-Degree Mother Hunger. Fear of abandonment, difficulty sleeping, eating disorders, mood problems, and difficulty finding meaning in life are all part of complex post-traumatic stress and Third-Degree Mother Hunger. Addiction to something or someone can feel like a life raft. So can suicidal thoughts and self-harm.

As adults, women with Third-Degree Mother Hunger often suffer physical symptoms as well as psychological symptoms of trauma. Physical symptoms may include chronic back and neck pain, fibromyalgia, migraines, digestive problems, spastic colon or irritable bowel syndrome, allergies, thyroid and other endocrine disorders, chronic fatigue, and some forms of asthma. These symptoms may explain some of the remarkable increases in medical issues uncovered by Dr. Felitti in the original ACE study. For those with Third-Degree Mother Hunger, there is no body-based experience of comfort or safety, because the person designed to be our source of comfort became our source of fear.

Misunderstood Signs of Complex Trauma

Although some mothers are cruel, it's my belief that maternal cruelty is not a calculated desire to hurt one's child. Abusive mothers have often endured their own trauma that is inherited, passed from one generation to the next. However, if you are the daughter of a cruel mother, the *reason* she was mean doesn't matter to the little girl inside you. It never made sense while you were growing up, and it may not make sense now. It just feels awful. Even if you understand that your mother's cruelty wasn't purposeful, the pain she caused you is real, it's deep, and it needs repair.

Third-Degree Mother Hunger comes from having a compromised mother who frightened you during the years you depended on her. Instead of nurturing, protecting, or guiding you, she yelled, hit, shamed, or abandoned you. As a result, your relationship with yourself and others is devastated. Terrible mood swings startle you and anyone close to you. You have periodic bursts of energy but no direction for it. Nights are scary and sleep is difficult. Inside, you carry a haunting confusion about your basic needs and wants and a deep feeling of homelessness that creates a burning need for emotional escape.

Mystified by the constellation of behaviors that mimic personality disorders, well-meaning professionals aren't always able to help. Perhaps you found temporary relief from a clinical diagnosis or medication, but it rarely lasts. This is because a diagnosis of a personality disorder misses the original wound underneath your behaviors. Without a sensitive, well-trained response to the root cause of your reactivity, you still wake up with disturbing, relentless symptoms. You still have signs of a heartbreak that no one can see and no one wants to talk about.

Surviving a dangerous mother is an unspeakable trauma that is difficult to recognize. Perhaps we cannot see it because deep inside each of us is a little person who remembers the vulnerability of being totally dependent, and the idea that a mother could betray this dependency is terrifying. It strikes a primitive fear in our mammal brain. The helplessness and devastation of life with Third-Degree Mother Hunger is why I believe having a dangerous, frightening mother is the worst childhood adversity of all.

Betrayal

We know that kids who experience horrifying events and adversity don't all develop symptoms of traumatic stress. That's because of one determining factor: if a familiar, consistent adult can help make sense of what's happening, kids can tolerate adversity. But when a mother is the source of fear, her love *is* the traumatic event. And there is no way to make sense of this. Danger fuses with love. Instincts for self-preservation surrender to the overarching need for bonding, creating what's known as a *betrayal bond* with the mother.

When a mother's love is threatening, your body remembers the pain at a molecular level. An abusive mother generates traumatic stress, because your coping capacity becomes overwhelmed and you are too young to protect yourself. Since a mother's love is your primary defense from adversity, when she is the threat, her care is a profound relational betrayal.

To bond with an unkind mother, our merciful imagination works overtime to create a different mother from the one we have. We create one who loves us, one who is taking care of us, one who isn't betraying our vulnerability. Our brain designs a different mother to help us cope with constant fear. Sadly, in service to bonding, these necessary brain changes create long-term personality problems. Surviving Third-Degree Mother Hunger may have left you with automatic dissociative patterns, chronic shame, and the propensity to land in relationships with others who betray you.

Acknowledging Abuse

Describing an abusive mother is not easy. We don't like to think of mothers who hurt their children. The idea is so abhorrent that our collective denial protects us from the knowledge that it happens. Periodically, we read tragedies of maternal neglect in the news or see a movie where a destructive mother is portrayed, but for the most part, we deny that mothers harm their daughters.

Frequently, women send me e-mails after learning about Third-Degree Mother Hunger, describing their own experiences of it:

I feel like I should be happy, but I'm not. I feel an ache and a deep, deep sorrow for what never was and will never be. It's hard to remember and know that I'm lovable, even though I wasn't loved. I feel profoundly sad and alone, while simultaneously celebrating my own ability to mother, love, nurture. It feels like a hidden aching and gaping wound that I should be over by now, but that I will carry within all the days of my life.

Or this one:

My own mother burned me at the stake and blames me for lighting the fire. Long, long story. I haven't had contact in over a decade. I wish that pain would go away.

For purposes of understanding and healing Third-Degree Mother Hunger, it's helpful to talk about different types of abuse, because for many of you, these behaviors might seem normal. It's impossible to develop new protective skills if you aren't aware of how you were hurt and where you need help.

Emotional Abuse

Defining emotional abuse is complicated because we can't actually see the injury. To start, let's think of what we've already covered about infant needs. Since inadequate nurturance and protection changes brain structures, their absence is harmful. Lack of nurturance and protection is neglectful, and neglect is a form of emotional abuse. Neglect is sometimes a "quiet" form of abuse—it's not obvious, because it happens privately. This explains why it can take decades to identify, understand, and recover from this type of emotional abuse.

As we covered in Chapter 7, when a mother treats her daughter as a friend, this is also a form of emotional abuse. The mother who tells her child, "You're everything to me . . . I don't know what I'd do without you," isn't mothering. She's creating a confusing emotional bind for her child. A child hears these words and might feel special (*I'm the favorite*), which feels great at first but sets her up for disappointment and alienates her from the rest of the family. She might also feel afraid (*Is Mom okay?*) or excessively dutiful (*I belong to Mom; it's my job to protect her and keep her happy*). This child may grow up to feel she's betraying her mother if she has other interests or friends or wants to move away.

Verbal insults are "noisy" forms of emotional abuse. Cruel comments such as "I wish you'd never been born" or "You're stupid" impact the body like a physical slap.

More subtle, nuanced forms of emotional abuse, like a dismissive glance or rejected hug, are challenging to identify, but also leave a scar, because it's the most fundamental form of rejection. When a mother rejects or degrades her daughter, there may be no witness. Being left alone to make sense of the negative feelings intensifies the injury.

Emotionally abusive mothers rarely repair the hurt they cause, and the lack of acknowledgment is what causes an enduring psychological trauma.

The definition of *trauma* comes from a Greek word that means "wound," "an injury to the body, mind, or spirit." Body, mind, and spirit are all involved with emotions. Obviously, we can't see an injury to the mind or spirit the way we can see a cut or bruise. Emotional trauma is difficult to quantify for this exact reason. But emotional abuse is psychologically traumatic because it betrays a fundamental role of parenting: it violates trust. Without the ability to trust a mother's love, daughters have no idea how to love themselves.

Missing an emotional safety net, the developing young brain focuses on finding safety elsewhere instead of playing, relaxing, or bonding with others. In this way, an emotionally abusive mother distorts her daughter's inner life, creating personality adaptations that may bring on future trouble. For example, girls with abusive mothers have difficulty making friends. They struggle to trust. Prolonged activation of the stress response system (from lack of trust) disrupts developing brain architecture, making it difficult to manage emotions, moods, and thoughts. Girls with Third-Degree Mother Hunger feel unsafe and act like it. Sometimes cold and brittle, other times childlike and docile, women with Third-Degree Mother Hunger have frozen, fractured emotional development. This explains why daughters of abusive mothers may be unpredictable or untrustworthy. Reacting to life with the mind of someone young and afraid is the legacy of abuse; not an indication of character or value.

Physical Abuse

Physical contact between a mother and daughter is part of nurturance. A mother's touch is as necessary as food. But when a mother's touch is disrespectful or aggressive, it leaves a damaging impact that can last a lifetime. The case of Caroline is a good example.

As a little girl, Caroline remembered being afraid she might drown when her mother washed her hair. "The water was up my nose, I couldn't breathe, but she kept holding my head under." Caroline cried and protested, but it didn't stop her mother's aggression.

As an adult, Caroline has difficulty washing her own hair and typically goes many days without bathing. She also avoids medical care. She has an intense fear of hospitals and needles.

Caroline suffered multiple childhood illnesses and remembers waking up on "doctor days" with a heavy feeling, her body tight and cold. She hated the antiseptic smell of the clinic, and the moment she got inside, she would begin to panic, scanning for an escape, but her mother would firmly grip her arm. "Stop worrying," she would insist, tightening her hold.

Let's pause for a moment here. Think of the last time you were scared. Did it help when someone told you to stop worrying?

Caroline remembered looking up to her mother's face, seeing furrowed brows, pursed lips, and a cold stare. "Behave, you're embarrassing me," her mother growled. On one particular visit, when the doctor arrived, Caroline broke free of her mother's grasp. She couldn't remember where she was going, only that she was running. Her mother caught up with her and spanked her in the middle of the clinic hall.

Recalling this incident in a session, Caroline's mind goes blank, even as her eyes fill with tears. Her resourceful brain dissociates to escape the still-raw pain. I cover her lap with a gravity blanket and sit quietly on the floor beside her. After a few moments, her body begins to settle. When her breathing returns to normal, I get up and slowly begin gentle eye movement desensitization (EMDR) to help her metabolize the terror stuck in her body.

Caroline's mother's aggressive, intrusive handling would qualify as physical abuse by any measure and created a third-degree relational burn that Caroline is to this day working to heal.

Spanking

For a long time, spanking has been considered an appropriate way to "train" a child, but, finally, this is ending. While spanking might appear effective in the short term, there is no existing study to support the idea that spanking or physical pain leads to long-term positive outcomes. The research suggests that parents who spank their children are actually unable to regulate their own emotions. Spanking is a shortcut, an emotional bypass from parental discomfort, anger, or helplessness. Parents justify spanking in all kinds of ways, but it is an abuse of power. Spanking leads to fear, aggression, humiliation, and withdrawal in children. Spanking a child is the opposite of nurturing, protecting, or guiding.

In a study of children exposed to routine, painful medical procedures, such as allergy shots or blood draws, the anticipatory distress before the painful procedure intensified pain and anxiety.[13] From this study, it's understandable that when a child expects a spanking, anticipatory distress becomes part of the overwhelming experience. When spankings are frequent, a child may develop anticipatory distress as she predicts or awaits the abuse. She gets jittery, jumpy, or withdrawn. Stomachaches or headaches are normal. During a spanking, physiological reactions such as heart pounding, vomiting, and even loss of bowel or bladder control can occur. Spanking creates toxic stress for a child and for the siblings who watch, eroding trust and safety in a family.[14] Children who were spanked suffer long-term symptoms, such as depression, anxiety, and emotional distress.[15]

If you were spanked as a child, you may feel disgusted by your body. It may be difficult to care for yourself (including pursuing medical care, dental care, regular exercise, and healthy nutrition) because your body has been a battleground. You may find it validating to know that the American Academy of Pediatrics recommends that parents avoid spanking children for any reason, and some researchers are fighting to include spanking on the list of adverse childhood experiences.[16]

Sexual Abuse

I don't think anyone is confused about what sexual abuse is. However, we assume that most mothers protect their daughters from such violations. It's unimaginable that a mother could participate in sexually endangering her daughter. We know that childhood sexual abuse leads to many forms of addiction and self-destructive behavior. And more than the abuse itself, women mourn the fact that no one protected them. Their mothers didn't help them or, in some cases, refused to believe them—particularly when the offending person was someone the mother loved. Mothers who turn the other way when their boyfriends, their husbands, or their own parents sexually violate their daughters are part of the abuse.

We may be aware that sexual abuse happens to little girls, but the fact that a mother could be the perpetrator is unthinkable. In her book *A Mother's Touch*, Julie Brand writes about being molested by her mother. She talks about how her mother fondled her during naptime. The abuse felt strange, but because there was no force, she never considered it abuse. But the long-term, enduring impact of sexual abuse isn't just about physical pain. Not all sexual abuse physically hurts. Mothers who misuse their daughters for affection and touch they need are at risk for this type of abuse.

When pain is involved, the offense is clear. Julie Brand shares about the humiliating weekly enemas she was forced to endure. "I would have to strip naked and lie facedown on my stomach on a bath towel on the linoleum floor. . . . I remember her holding me firmly with the weight of her foot on my back. She would not let me get up until she decided that I had endured enough."[17] Violations of a sexual nature often lead to a full rejection of one's sexuality, or risky sexual behavior.

Battered Woman Syndrome

Intimate relationships marked by frequent rage explosions are frightening places to be. Psychotherapist Lenore Walker developed the concept of *battered woman syndrome* in the late 1970s to describe the unique behaviors and emotions that develop when a person experiences abuse at the hands of an intimate partner. According to the National Coalition Against Domestic Violence, victims of domestic violence share symptoms that may include:

- Feeling isolated, anxious, depressed, or helpless
- Feeling embarrassed of judgment and stigmatization
- Feeling love for the person harming them and believing they will change
- Feeling emotionally withdrawn and lacking support from family and friends
- Denying that anything is wrong or excusing the person who is abusing them
- Having moral or religious reasons for staying in the relationship[18]

Since a mother is our first intimate partner and she has access to our body at all times, her cruelty is a form of domestic violence. If she handles us aggressively or directs her rage at us, we experience unimaginable terror. Carrying symptoms like the victims of intimate partner violence, we struggle to make friends or find a place to belong. We feel inherently bad. Almost unanimously, victims of partner violence believe domestic abuse is their fault. Daughters of abusive mothers do too.

Little girls with abusive mothers rarely talk about the abuse. In fact, they generally don't identify abusive maternal behavior at all. It just feels normal. Adaptations to intimate violence change the brain's ability to make sense of what's happening by prioritizing safety over learning and communicating.[19]

Psychobiological adaptations to fear brought on by maternal abuse can be long-lasting, complicating relationships for a daughter throughout her life. The NCADV explains how a person who has been through intimate partner abuse will have symptoms long after leaving the relationship. Symptoms of domestic violence include sleep problems; intrusive flashbacks and feelings of terror; avoiding topics or situations that are reminders; feelings of hopelessness, rage, and worthlessness; and panic attacks.[20]

Daughters with Third-Degree Mother Hunger share these symptoms. They idealize the abuser (their mother), believe they deserve the abuse, and suffer a humiliating loss of self-worth. Some professionals use the term *pathological accommodation* to describe what happens when a child learns to survive abuse. Accommodating and appeasing a frightening mother is an adaptation to inescapable fear. While tending to an abusive mother's moods, a daughter loses access to her own sensations and agency.[21] Pathological accommodation is the biological freeze response in action, which may explain the physical ailments that accompany Third-Degree Mother Hunger. A body that is frozen hurts.

Disorganized Attachment: The Lost Attachment Style

Women with Third-Degree Mother Hunger rarely felt *safely* attached to anyone growing up. Early on, they adapted to a frightening mother, and the bond was traumatic. Trauma bonds—strong emotional attachments between an abused person and her abuser—form when the human neuropathway for danger and attachment are activated simultaneously and damage the attachment system.[22] When a traumatic bond forms between a mother and her daughter, this toxic connection impacts all other relationships in the daughter's life. Fear destroys the attachment system, creating disorganized attachment, or Third-Degree Mother Hunger. Disorganized attachment is the potent legacy of a harmful mother.

In Chapter 2, we talked about the attachment categories *secure, anxious,* and *avoidant* that come from Mary Ainsworth's important research. Ainsworth actively measured John Bowlby's principles of attachment by examining reunion behavior between caregivers and toddlers in her now famous experiment called *strange situation.*[23] In a later study, Ainsworth's student Mary Main found signs of a fourth attachment category. Main noticed how some children without secure attachment behaved differently than their anxious or avoidant peers when their mother left and reentered the room. When the mother returned, these little ones would first run toward her, but then pull or run away. Some curled up in a ball or hit the mother. The first impulse to seek comfort is evident, but as the mother approached, the child became afraid. These children were "disorganized" and disoriented, as demonstrated by confused expressions, freezing, or wandering.[24] Judy Garland and Édith Piaf were both living with disorganized attachment. Their symptoms followed them into adulthood and grew more intense with time (and lack of therapeutic intervention) as both women raged at lovers, threw tantrums in restaurants, and struggled to hold on to successful careers.

When life gets intense, women with Third-Degree Mother Hunger melt or rage. Melting or collapsing is a freeze response. Raging is the fight-or-flight response. Certain bodily signals (such as smells, sounds, or touch) become reminders of early helplessness and quickly set off impulsivity and dissociation. When activated, women with Third-Degree Mother Hunger struggle to soothe themselves or identify something or someone who could.

Deep in their bones, women with disorganized attachment believe no one is safe. Living this way requires some form of self-medicating. Judy Garland and Édith Piaf both used drugs, alcohol, and romance to numb the pain of their childhood. In spite of health problems, loss of respect, and trouble singing, their addictions escalated. Their stories aren't unique. Most women with disorganized attachment work too much, spend too much, or eat too much. Some deprive themselves of basic needs. Fleeting emotional highs mask the pain of not belonging anywhere or to anyone. Generally, their first experience of human safety and genuine warmth comes from a professional who is trained to work with complex developmental trauma.

Dissociation

When a threat exceeds our coping abilities, nature protects us from overwhelming fear through the body and mind mercifully taking us away from reality. Dissociation, a parasympathetic process of downregulating the nervous system in response to impending danger, is a survival reaction. We literally and temporarily leave awareness as our breathing slows down and we become immobile. This is nature's way of preparing for death. It's not a conscious process. It's automatic. Dissociation happens when we feel there is no other option in the face of a threat.

As infants or children, the reality of a frightening mother presents us with an impossible dilemma: the person who could soothe our fear is causing it. The only way to cope is to disappear.

When maternal threats are constant, so is dissociation. Dissociation becomes a way to hide from intolerable things that are happening, as we saw in Caroline's session with me. Dissociating might feel like tunnel vision, a hazy sense of time, a tingling in the ears, or a dreamlike sense of being someone else or somewhere else. One of my favorite descriptions of dissociation is from Marissa Korbel's article in *Harper's Bazaar* called "Sometimes You Make Your Rapist Breakfast":

> Dissociation sounds scary, but it doesn't feel bad. Sometimes it feels like sliding into a warm, cozy bed. A secret, safe place where I can stay as long as I want. It's the coming back that breaks me open. That's when I always cry.[25]

This is why many women avoid healing Third-Degree Mother Hunger—the lurking avalanche of fear is just too awful.

Third-Degree Mother Hunger comes from relational fear without relational repair. During our formative years, fear without repair creates lifelong changes in the brain. Herein lies the essence of complex trauma. When a mother can't acknowledge, apologize for, and amend her harm, fear changes a child's brain functions, leaving her with a blurred sense of identity and vague feelings about reality.

Dissociating protected you when you needed it, but the habit makes past events difficult to recall. Rest assured, your body holds the story:

> Cognitive processing is inextricably linked with our bodies. . . . All early relational dynamics with primary caregivers, traumatic or nontraumatic, serve as blueprints for the child's developing cognition and belief systems, and these belief systems influence the posture, structure and movement of the body."[26]

Tucked away from conscious awareness, like it or not, the memoir of your life is in your body—silently informing physical and mental well-being—trying to get your attention through body aches, regular nightmares, and chronic anxiety.

At the mercy of a cold, aggressive, or abandoning mother, a daughter must believe that her mother will change. Dissociation permits this persistent hope, almost like a fantasy. As children, some of you created imaginary friends, different parents, or a charming prince to buffer fear. Fantasizing is a powerful way to endure intolerable feelings when there is no escape. When danger is ongoing, dissociation goes into overdrive. Nature's merciful design, keeping you from having to reckon with overwhelming reality, hides data that could be useful, such as information about how to detect a dangerous person. When the dangerous person is your mother, what good is the information? Since you couldn't leave her, your brain constrains awareness with an emotional eye patch. In this way, dissociation is a lifesaver.

When we are helpless, dissociation buffers unbearable reality, but it also creates a division between the self that is going through life (attending school, learning to read, making friends, playing sports) and the self that is holding unexpressed fear, shame, and anger. In essence, we divide into parts. We have an external part who goes through the motions of life and an internal self who hides. Sometimes, we don't know which self is real.[27]

Anticipatory trauma—rehearsing how to cope with the next spanking or coming home from school or the next drink Mom pours—explains why fear may cause immobility. Feeling slow, stuck, or frozen is the body's way of preparing for assault. In addition to dissociating or daydreaming, the brain buffers fear and powerlessness by freezing—preparing for death.[28] Working together, dissociation and paralysis prepare the body for unavoidable pain.

Betrayal Blindness

In spite of decades of evidence that a mother can't or won't change harmful behaviors, daughters cling to hope. I call this *pathological hope*. Pathological hope starts as a protective measure—a way to endure adversity. But over time, pathological hope may keep women stuck in painful relational cycles with others. Most don't notice the nature of pathological hope because the brain adapted so early. Daughters of abusive mothers have been fighting to be noticed, fighting to be protected, fighting to be nurtured, and fighting for an apology most of their lives.

Pathological hope has amazing staying power. The enduring nature of wishful thinking could relate to a psychological phenomenon known as betrayal blindness. Jennifer Freyd, Ph.D., has spent years researching the complex biological processes that explain why some of us get stuck in abusive relationships. Freyd coined the term *betrayal blindness* to explain how adults can forget or simply not know when we're being hurt in an intimate relationship. She explains that "because we are dependent on the betrayer—our next best defense is to block out awareness of the betrayal; in other words, a kind of mental freeze (betrayal blindness) is our next best option."[29] Freyd helps us understand how this psychological adaptation to danger is based on an extreme need to keep a situation intact, whether "maintaining a marriage, keeping a family together, or holding on to one's position in a community."[30]

It's logical that betrayal blindness helps a child survive a frightening mother. Blindness serves the greater purpose of attachment. Since the needs of human attachment override defensive needs, the biological mechanisms that let us bond with a scary mother become part of our personality. A survival personality with little self-awareness forms, as betrayal blindness protects us from knowing that we have become experts at living with and loving a dangerous person. Blind to our betrayal, we don't realize that loving someone is now fused with pity or duty. We feel sorry for our fragile, abusive mother. Sometimes we comfort her after she loses control, hits us, and feels guilty. Or we feel responsible—we try to save her from an abusive partner or a bill collection agency. We become *her* protector.

Daughters who nurture and protect their mothers are appeasing them. Nature's "appease" response wires us to behave this way when we have nowhere else to go, creating a bond with our mother in spite of being afraid of her. "Children are programmed to be fundamentally loyal to their caretakers, even if they are abused by them. Terror increases the need for attachment, even if the source of comfort is also the source of terror."[31] In this way, betrayal becomes wired with love. This is not a conscious experience. We don't have control over early adaptations to fear. We need our mother even when she yells at us, pulls our hair, or tells us we're fat.

Appeasing an abusive mother sets up a lifetime of relational confusion. And we may find ourselves in one destructive relationship after another.

The Biology of Appeasement

Dr. Stephen Porges's polyvagal theory, like Dr. Shelly Taylor's tend-and-befriend work, explains how our social nervous system is built to bond with others, especially during adversity.[32] This is a human response to fear. We need to "befriend" when we are threatened by someone or something. The inherent tragedy of Third-Degree Mother Hunger is that the mother *is* the adversity. And even if Mom is dangerous, a daughter will bond to her. Befriending and appeasing behaviors keep a daughter near her mother. Appeasing emerges from hopeless terror—from knowing that there is nowhere else to go. This is not a choice; this is biology.

Biological responses to danger are meant for emergencies, not for routine survival, and certainly not to endure a frightening mother. Maternal cruelty brings on the emergency response system, rapidly changing a daughter's developing brain architecture. High levels of cortisol, the stress hormone, damage brain regions meant for social interaction.

For those of you interested in the brain, you may already know how stress impacts the temporal lobe—specifically the amygdala and hippocampus. Stress irritates the functioning of the amygdala, where empathy develops.[33] Cortisol poisons the hippocampus, which makes sense of incoming data and memory processing. The brain is adapting, keeping the necessary biological processes going, like our heartbeat and breathing, but filtering out less critical processes, like memory and empathy. During a stressful event or moment, the brain literally ignores information secondary to survival.

Over time, unused brain neurons and synaptic connections disappear. Scientists call this sophisticated neurological process *pruning*.[34]

Imagine for a moment what the brain must do to ignore (and eventually prune) the neurological processes that identify a dangerous mother? It must compartmentalize fear somewhere outside your consciousness so that bonding can happen. Over time, the brain shrinks danger signals, like a mother's shrill voice or furrowed brow, so you can tolerate her proximity. Pruning alters perception and protects you when you are small and dependent, but over time, your innate ability to detect or discern risky situations is twisted. In this way, neuroception is altered, which is why exposure to early betrayal puts you at a greater risk of further victimization.

Maternal abuse is a devastating betrayal because not only do you miss out on essential nurturance, protection, and guidance, but your neuroception and protective instincts are also damaged. Since you are adapted to danger, situations that would frighten a regular person don't raise a red flag for you. You know how to bond with others who may betray you. You might even be bored by people who don't.

Toxic Shame

The toxic shame that results from maternal abuse convinces us we are defective. This is not the kind of shame that you feel when you hurt someone's feelings or the shame that tells you it's not a good idea to flirt with your sister's partner. Toxic shame makes you question your right to be here. Toxic shame mires your soul in a tar pit of insecurity.

My hope is that understanding Third-Degree Mother Hunger will reduce the shame you are carrying. You aren't defective or broken. Toxic shame is an inherited type of shame that has *nothing* to do with you. You could be carrying shame that belongs to your mother, like the shame she didn't feel when she mistreated you.

Carried shame feels heavy and thick, like an unwanted, dirty blanket you can't get out from under. Relational psychotherapist and author Patricia DeYoung says toxic shame is "lodged somewhere deeper than words, a 'sickness of the soul,' with even less form than a feeling."[35] For this reason, it's hard to identify or discuss toxic shame. Over time, toxic shame fuels forms of self-abuse like cutting, starving, addiction, and isolation.

Sometimes toxic shame masquerades as pseudo confidence or an inflated sense of superiority: a cover-up for feeling awful. You feel pathetic but certainly don't want anyone to know, so you're quick to judge others before they judge you. For a minute, this makes you feel better, until you eat a package of Girl Scout cookies behind the closet door or get drunk at a company party and behave poorly. Afterward, the voice that says *I am disgusting and useless and no one should ever talk to me again* starts talking. And it usually sounds like your mother. But remember: Your personality developed to survive your mother's lack of care. It's not your true self.

Specialized Treatment

Palliative care, specialized treatment for difficult health issues, focuses on providing relief rather than a cure. I think of Third-Degree Mother Hunger as a difficult health issue, and a palliative care paradigm gives me a compass for supporting women with third-degree trauma. I look to the work that is being done at Reconnect, Dr. Karol Darsa's treatment facility that incorporates diverse approaches for survivors, where adults receive care throughout the day and sessions may include art therapy, mindfulness, brainspotting, or EMDR. Each person has an opportunity for a psychiatric evaluation, as medication can be lifesaving for Third-Degree Mother Hunger. Palliative care is best when teams work together, as they do in Darsa's program, and when it includes holistic curative treatments in addition to traditional ones.

Healing Third-Degree Mother Hunger requires support from well-trained professionals who understand complex trauma, attachment, and sensorimotor psychotherapy. Pat Ogden, Ph.D., Ruth Lanius, M.D., Ph.D., and Janina Fisher, Ph.D., have developed methods to access and heal body memory that is deeper than words.[36]

Next Steps for Survivors of Third-Degree Mother Hunger

Healing Third-Degree Mother Hunger is a twofold process: First, you find words for the speechless terror you felt as a child. You are doing this right now. Reading this book gives you language for the disorganized heartbreak you've endured for so long. Second, if you haven't done so already, it's time to stop reaching for your mother, rest your weary soul, and grieve what is lost. In order for this to work, you need the company of someone who understands this unique pain and/or a clinician trained in and dedicated to healthy attachment. Your pain emerged from relational trauma, and it will only heal with healthy relational experiences.

As you uncover implicit memory (which can happen), the story of your mother's care will bring a greater capacity to love and protect yourself going forward. Healing involves integrating implicit memories and forming a coherent narrative about your relationship with her.

As you gain awareness, new behaviors may be necessary to protect yourself. For some of you, "divorcing" your mother will be part of healing this third-degree burn. You might start with a 30-day separation, disconnecting from contact via phone, text, social media . . . anywhere she can see or connect with you. As you practice new boundaries, creating safety for yourself, you are essentially coming out of a dissociative trance that you've been in most of your life. Emerging from constant dissociation means facing buried emotions. This is a good time to remember what your goal is: You are building secure attachment within yourself that was lost in your formative years. You are creating an internal home where you are safe and loved.

In the healing process, it's normal to feel terrified, angry, and very much alone. If you sometimes feel like a bad daughter, I hope this chapter stops that kind of thinking and relieves your burden.

Keep in mind that others have walked this journey before you, paving the way to a new, steady sense of self without the constant disappointment, heartache, and betrayal that comes from unhealthy maternal contact. As your body feels safe, overall emotional reactivity diminishes. You'll recover faster after a nightmare or an argument with someone you love. Gradually, dissociation loses its hold on you. Your suffering diminishes. And with the help of a trusted guide, you will build relational resilience. The heartache that has been your constant companion takes a break. In this new brain space, you can make better decisions about how and when to contact your mother—and whether contact is possible at all.

Living with untreated Third-Degree Mother Hunger is living with trauma. Facing it can feel risky and scary. Blocking pain is the brain's compassionate response to trauma; it compartmentalizes the memory. But it also makes life color-less and dull, and feeling authentic joy or finding meaning is a struggle.

Now that you have more awareness, healing can go deeper. You're beginning to reclaim lost maternal care as you release buried emotions and experience new warmth with others.

CHAPTER 9

HEALING MOTHER HUNGER

Curiosity may find you searching this chapter for answers. Frustrated and eager, you want the solution. I understand this. You want the pain to stop. You are tired of suffering. You want someone or something to make it better.

In the process of healing Mother Hunger, it's important to go at your own pace. Periodic pauses or steps backward are common. At times, you may wonder if you have made any progress at all, or if somehow you are betraying your mother by getting better. Some of you might wait until your mother is no longer living to do this work. That's okay. Whenever and however you decide to proceed is up to you. You are the architect now.

It's natural to feel afraid as you face this injury. Asking for help might be particularly difficult, because allowing someone to support you is a vulnerable position to be in. Even if you feel ready for guidance, the power imbalance between you and a helping professional reminds your unconscious of the fear that if someone really knows you, they can manipulate and control you. For these reasons, it's essential to find a therapist who understands attachment theory and who can gently pace your healing process.

As we learn more about the brain, new tools are emerging all the time that help us rewire areas impacted by trauma and adversity. There is new hope for healing a broken heart. Healing Mother Hunger means you have a chance to earn the secure attachment you missed early in life. While this goes faster when you have healthy relationships around you, new inner security can also grow from your own efforts.

Healing Mother Hunger has a rhythm of its own. Heartbreak can flare up whenever the wound is touched by a familiar song, a particular smell, a holiday, or a stray thought. When it does, ask yourself what hurts. Are you longing for affection? Are you feeling scared? Do you feel lost? As previously mentioned, Mother Hunger exists on a spectrum and relates to the essential maternal elements you were missing. Although there isn't a magic formula for healing Mother Hunger, identifying how you feel can direct how or where to start. How long it takes to feel secure within yourself will depend on the severity of missing maternal nurturance, protection, or guidance. If you missed all three, healing may take longer.

In addition to the healing exercises at the end of most chapters, this chapter has additional guidelines to help you feel more secure within yourself and with others.

- Identify your primary missing maternal needs. Do you crave affection and quality time from one special someone? You need more nurturance. Are you routinely anxious and afraid? You need more protection. Do you feel uninspired or lost? You need guidance.

- Understand what I call *apology ache*. We'll learn about this on page 176.

- Understand disenfranchised grief (page 180).

- Discover the benefits of a having a celestial mother (page 185).

- Find professional support. A qualified attachment-focused therapist can help regardless of where you are on the Mother Hunger spectrum. If you are facing Third-Degree Mother Hunger, a therapist who is trauma informed is critical.

Earned Secure Attachment

You are designed to heal from illness and injury, but until you pinpoint the issue, the brain isn't sure exactly what to do. Naming the pain of Mother Hunger gives your body a compass that directs your inner wisdom. Your body appreciates this. The roadblock to well-being has been removed so you can focus on creating an "earned" secure attachment. Whether your dominant attachment style is avoidant or anxious or you land somewhere on the spectrum of disorganized, earned secure attachment can relieve the intensity of your heartache. Earning security comes from developing a connection deep within yourself, and if you are healing Third-Degree Mother Hunger, with someone else who is invested in your mental health and well-being.

Earning security comes from finding new ways to self-nurture, building authentic protection, and creating a coherent story about your formative years. I realize this sounds clinical and laborious. The truth is that although it's possible to create a healthier attachment style, it takes considerable effort to grow new pathways in your brain. Like beginning a new exercise routine, the first days are the worst. You're tired, off-balance, and unsure it will work. But with practice, you gain strength, momentum, and confidence. Healing Mother Hunger is similar.

You may find yourself feeling resentful as you think of the work ahead. That's okay. Resentment is natural. Earning secure attachment is a lot to juggle while you're working, studying, or caring for others. It seems like an unfair burden. And you might feel tired just reading about it. You might also be confused because missing maternal elements are deeply buried beneath protective amnesia. You may wonder, *What did I miss?* If you aren't sure, this is a good time to get support. Your missing needs are waiting for attention, but since early maternal messages are imprinted before language or explicit memory, they are harder to find than others. A trauma-trained somatic therapist can be incredibly helpful in uncovering these lost treasures.

Healing Mother Hunger doesn't always require clinical support, just like getting in shape doesn't always require a trainer or a gym. But if John Bowlby, the father of attachment theory, were here, he might encourage you to have a therapist anyway, because "the therapist's role is analogous to that of a mother who provides her child with a secure base from which to explore the world."[1]

Why Does Therapy Work?

Earning secure attachment comes from replacing the three essential maternal elements that you didn't have. To help your brain do this, you need a sense of history. How did you get here? Think back to your earliest memories with your mother. Was she affectionate with you? Could you rely on her when you were afraid? Do you think she was happy? Did she inspire you? Learning your story puts you in touch with the missing pieces so you can put them back together. With a story that explains your behavior and your feelings, energy for new decisions, dreams, and goals appears. Renewed focus is a sign that your attachment style is healing.

Healing happens by knowing what you *didn't* have so you can fill your empty spirit with the right ingredients. We simply can't change what we don't know. Knowing happens in two ways: cognitively and emotionally. Reading and learning about Mother Hunger is cognitive. This is your left brain in action. Cognitive awareness is the first step.

But to create lasting change, you must *feel* the wound—the sickening emptiness that yearns to be nurtured, protected, or guided. Most of us can't feel this pain without help. After a lifetime of protecting ourselves, the brain simply won't let go unless we are safe and supported. Your lovely brain is waiting for you to find a guide—someone with no other agenda than to help you find yourself.

Mother Hunger is a right brain wound. Right brain language is expressed body to body, in the quality of eye contact, voice tones, and rhythms of response. Through the nonverbal interactions that happen with a competent, well-trained clinician, the right brain heals from "the music, not the words, of what passes between people."[2] This is how psychotherapy works and why I hope you find a supportive guide. But this is also how healthy connection works. If you have a close friend or a trustworthy partner, some forms of Mother Hunger can heal without professional support because the relational wound is receiving relational care.

Replacing Lost Maternal Nurturance

If you aren't used to being nurtured, it can feel strange when you begin caring for yourself in healthy ways. You might feel uneasy, annoyed, or disgusted. This is *normal*.

Here are some excellent ways to help you replace the missing maternal element of nurturance:

- Soak in a tub or saltwater tank: the water is like a human hug.

- Seek regular bodywork that is trauma sensitive.

- Practice restorative yoga to ease emotional wounds stuck in your body.

- Try a gravity blanket when you go to bed or rest on the couch.

- Listen to a mindful podcast like Tara Brach or *On Being* with Krista Tippett.

- Walk in nature where silence can find you.

- Light your favorite scented candle.

- Drink noncaffeinated herbal tea at night.

- Take naps when possible. Curl up with something soft, like a favorite pillow or pet.

- Sleep when you can, but if sleeping is a way to avoid things, try other ways to nurture yourself. You wouldn't let a child sleep all day.

If your mother is alive, it might be tempting to go to her for nurturance. However, if she couldn't provide affection or tenderness when you were small, she still might not be able to. It's a natural impulse to want her to nurture you. Part of healing Mother Hunger might mean that you take a break from reaching for her—at least until you have a better idea about healthy ways to connect with yourself.

21 Days to Detox and Connect with Yourself

For 21 days, I encourage you to detox from regular exposure to your mother (or thoughts of your mother). To do so,
you'll want to practice healthy nurturance and avoid texting,
talking, or being with her. For three weeks, try the following:

- Feed yourself as you would a young child. Avoid
  sugar, caffeine, and processed foods.

- Write down your thoughts and feelings as you
  notice them. This is one of the *hardest* healing
  tasks, but it's essential.

- Make sleep a priority. Apps like Calm or Insight
  Timer are helpful for sleepless nights.

- Limit your exposure to social media.
  Check e-mail only when necessary during
  the workday.

- Practice spending time alone, *without* a
  romantic partner, family member, or friend
  to entertain, comfort, or distract you. Try
  practicing solitude in a conscious, present way.

- Put devices away at night. If you use your
  device to listen to a sleep or meditation podcast,
  set it to airplane mode or "do not disturb."

- If all of this seems impossible, and you keep
  reaching for your mother only to find yourself
  hurt and disappointed again, consider seeking
  the help of a licensed therapist. A support
  group can be extremely helpful if you currently
  have addictive habits. Some groups have
  phone meetings as well as local meetings. I
  recommend the following:

- Overeaters Anonymous (OA): oa.org
- Sex and Love Addicts Anonymous (SLAA): slaafws.org
- Adult Children of Alcoholics (ACA): adultchildren.org
- Alcoholics Anonymous (AA): aa.org

Replacing Lost Maternal Protection

If you weren't protected as a child, anxiety feels normal. Earning secure attachment means making your life as safe as possible so that you can reset your baseline. Your body has no idea what relaxation feels like, because you've been alert and ready for danger most of your life.

The previous nurturance strategies help with protection too, because they are calming. But here are some additional things to consider:

- Avoid movies and shows with violence.
- Turn off the news.
- Listen to your intuition if someone or something feels "off."
- Calm your overactive amygdala with relaxation techniques. (See the previous nurturance recommendations and the alternate nostril breathing exercise on page 115.)
- Move your body gently. Exercise motivates a sleepy, dissociated nervous system.
- Spend time with safe people.
- Listen to educational podcasts about attachment. *Therapist Uncensored* is a good one.

- Conscious, healthy dissociation soothes fear. It's helpful to find ways to turn off your fear brain so your body can relax. Happy movies help. In this way, media can be a mindful distraction instead of a mind-numbing escape.

If your mother is enmeshing, as we saw with Malabar in *Wild Game*, protection includes establishing new boundaries with her. To learn how to do this, you might need to avoid her for a period of time. Physical and emotional space allows you to experience your own emotions in ways you never have before. Free to flow, your emotions can teach you what you need to do to feel safe around your mother.

Replacing Lost Maternal Guidance

We grow up breathing in parental expectations, so many of us unconsciously create a life that reflects their values instead of our own. The hopes parents have for their children are commonly a mix of overt goals and covert ones—the ones they don't say out loud. These messages can be contradictory and confusing for you. For example, your mother may have told you to be anything you want, but she only encouraged your brothers to pursue higher learning. Or maybe your mother felt threatened by the idea that you might become successful and leave her, so she discouraged your talents.

When you feel there's an invisible wall between you and the life you want, objective guidance may help you. You need a guide who can uncover the hidden contracts you have with your mother (or other caregivers) that are holding you back. Such hidden contracts might be internalized lessons that whisper *Be happy, but not happier than I am* or *Get married so I don't have to take care of you anymore* or *Make a lot of money so someday you can take care of me . . .*

An Exercise in Closeness

I help women locate missing maternal needs with a simple but powerful exercise. You can try this with a trusted friend.

Before diving in, we do some preparatory work to build trust and warmth in a safe therapeutic space. Then I ask my client to think of me as her mother. I reassure her that we can stop at any time. When she is ready, I stand up and walk to the center of the room, about four feet from her. Here's an example of a typical interaction:

KM: I'm your mother now.

I pause and wait until her eyes grow dim. Then, slowly, I take two steps forward. I watch. If she softens or leans toward me, I step forward a bit more. I pause and wait. As she relaxes, I step back to the first position and watch. If her posture sags or her face looks sad, this informs me that she didn't want me to go away.

KM: Do you want me to come back?

Client: Yes.

So I step forward again.

KM: How does this feel?

Client: Better.

KM: How did it feel when I stepped away from you?

Client: Sad . . . empty.

We just learned she prefers closeness. She will benefit from nurturance tasks to heal Mother Hunger.

Let's see what happens when I step toward a client and she winces or shrinks. In this case, I stop and back up two steps. I wait. I take note of her body language. If she's still uneasy, I take two more steps back to allow more space between us, watching her face, eyes, and posture for cues.

KM: Does this feel better?

Client: Yes.

KM: Okay, let's try something else.

I roll my desk chair between us, creating even more distance. I watch her expression. Sometimes her posture sags or she looks confused.

KM: How does the distance feel now?

Client: Too much . . . I don't like it.

KM: Okay.

I put the chair back where it came from and step forward again, but only two steps.

KM: Better?

Client: Yes, better.

I see her sigh of relief. We've found the sweet spot. She wants proximity with others, but not too much.

Sometimes, before a client can relax, I literally step outside the office door. When a client needs me to back away in this exercise, it's likely she didn't feel safe near her mother, suggesting that early protection was missing.

We each have a window of tolerance for the amount of human closeness we want. Throughout this quiet, powerful exercise, I'm assessing a client's attachment preferences: *How much is too much?* Understanding the unique configuration of your attachment style is like finding your inner compass or a map that directs your self-concept and feelings about others. Locating the inner compass driving your attachment needs illuminates your unconscious choices. Like finding a missing piece of jewelry—one you forgot you had—it's exciting. You don't want to lose it again.

To preserve the reclaimed gem, we discuss what just happened during this brief exercise and what it means. Such a conversation simultaneously activates the left brain and fortifies the right brain's new awareness. This is a step toward integrating implicit memory and explicit memory—making your story more personal and useful to you.

Apology Ache

Many of us are experts at acting like it's no big deal when someone hurts our feelings. We swallow pain to avoid conflict. Alternatively, some of us seek revenge when someone hurts us—we want them to feel as badly as we do. Most of us learn these strategies very young because when Mom hurt our feelings, she didn't apologize. We became masters at pretending we were okay when we didn't feel okay.

Apology ache is a term I created for the longing that your mother would see how much she hurt you and say "I'm sorry," the yearning for her to show remorse. You wait for an apology, hoping your pain will stop when she recognizes what she did wrong. But lots of mothers don't acknowledge their hurtful behaviors or apologize for them. They aren't sure how, or they feel too much shame, or they simply can't empathize.

The legacy of an unapologetic mother is incredibly hurtful. You might not recognize a sincere apology from someone else, because you never experienced one in your formative years. An apology is more than just the words *I'm sorry*, although those words are a great start. A true apology involves two things: recognition of your pain and repair efforts to mend hurtful behavior. Let's explore what an apology isn't:

- An apology is not an excuse. Anyone who follows up the words "I'm sorry" with the word "but" should make you nervous. "I'm sorry I hit you, but you need to stop _____ (whining, arguing, pouting, etc.)" or "I'm sorry I _____ (yelled at you, walked away, punished you, etc.), but you are just so difficult."

- An apology is not a denial. If someone tries to talk you out of your reality, that's not an apology. That's a way to avoid feeling remorse. Words like "Was it really that bad?" or "You're being too sensitive" add insult to injury. This type of apology asks you to ignore how you feel and adds shame to the hurt. Shaming efforts hide behind false apologies, like when someone suggests, "I'm sorry you feel that way," as if your feelings happened in a vacuum. Not only is this pseudo apology unhelpful, but if you were hurt before, now you're probably mad too.

- Apologies are not manipulative. If someone apologizes from a place of self-pity, they want your forgiveness without earning it. It might sound like, "I'm such a mess, I can't help it when I _____ (drink too much, check out other women, work too late, forget your birthday); it's just the way I am . . . " This is not an apology.

A manipulative mother might apologize like this: "I'm sorry I hit you. But you really made me mad. When you act that way, I can't help it . . ." She starts crying. "But I'm sorry . . . I love you; please come here and give me a hug." This type of apology is toxic; it puts the blame on the victim. When a mother blames you for her behavior, she is reacting from her own unexamined powerlessness. She distorts the truth of what is happening. You did not and do not cause her to hurt you.

A real apology might look like this: "I see that my drinking has upset you. I've been late to pick you up from school. I've been moody and unkind. This is not your fault. I'm so sorry that I've hurt you, and I will not drink anymore." This mother sees her impact and makes every effort to amend her behavior. She might seek professional help or attend 12-step meetings for addiction. In this way, she repairs and builds trust by her ongoing predictability. She stops the cycle that creates Mother Hunger.

When a mother apologizes in a healthy, adult manner, her humility and emotional maturity model what a trustworthy person looks like. A trustworthy mother is aware of her power, recognizes when she causes harm, and repairs the damage. Without treatment, however, abusive mothers do not have this capacity. If you have Third-Degree Mother Hunger, you may never receive a real apology from your mother. While this might be a hard thing to acknowledge, it's important to know that *you can heal* without her involvement. Her apology would certainly make it easier, but it's not necessary for mending your broken heart.

It's rare to give up hope for a mother to apologize or change if she is still alive. Instead of facing reality, you wait for the apology because that seems easier. Consider this a gentle invitation to try. Waiting for her apology delays your ability to grieve early losses, fill in missing pieces, and start enjoying your life. Waiting might be the biggest roadblock to healing. The necessary next step is facing grief.

Understanding Grief

In my practice, I listen to heartbreaking stories of abandonment and sorrow. Ridicule, neglect, and other toxic forms of maternal abuse add up to a lifetime of grief. While the stories are unique, there is a haunting similarity in each one—a type of eternal waiting and hoping for a mother to act like a mother. The fantasy of a loving mother hides behind the quest for something to fill the unnamed void.

Pathological hope is some of nature's finest work. Protective mechanisms meant for bonding wire us for hope even in the face of ample evidence that change is not forthcoming. So we hope for change instead of feeling what's real. Our brain protects us with emotional blinders until we are ready and able to face the legacy of missing maternal love. Busy orchestrating the perfect life or numbing out with too much of everything, we find the grief of Mother Hunger all too easy to avoid. In this way, grieving lost maternal love gets delayed until we have the proper support.

"Lack of safety and security during essential developmental periods, lack of responsiveness to [our] affective needs, and lack of recognition of [our] internal states of mind may lead to *dissociative states later in life, as well as to prolonged and complicated grief."*[3] Complicated grief is exactly how it sounds—complicated. Resistant to any particular stages of grief, the complicated sadness that is woven into the texture of Mother Hunger is deeply misunderstood and hard to reach. Perhaps this is also because the topic is taboo or because betrayal blindness keeps it hidden.

Grief related to Mother Hunger needs a framework that invites permission and acknowledgment for the complicated, unique ways each of us mourn the loss of maternal care. Are you grieving the mother you didn't have? Are you grieving how much this attachment injury has impacted your life? Are you grieving lost dreams? Are you grieving broken relationships and destructive behavior? Are you grieving all of these?

Disenfranchised Grief

When a parent loses a child, friends and family circle the wagons of support. When someone gets hurt in a car accident or faces cancer, communities respond with food, flowers, and visits. Suffering needs soothing. Heartbreak needs belonging. These efforts help us grieve. Without public validation, however, grieving stalls.

Dr. Kenneth Doka coined the term *disenfranchised grief* to explain a phenomenon that occurs when we experience a loss that cannot be openly acknowledged, like the grief that comes from terminating an affair. Since it was a secret and wasn't supposed to be happening, there's no support for the loss. Disenfranchised grief has nowhere to go.[4] When we don't have a name for what hurts or a place to talk about it, the grief process freezes.

When I read *A Mother's Reckoning*, Sue Klebold's memoir about being the mother of one of the Columbine killers, the concept of disenfranchised grief really hit home. I could feel her despair, her utter helplessness and shock. How could she mourn the loss of her son when he had harmed so many in such a horrific way? Who could she turn to for understanding? In the months following this tragedy, Sue felt like a frightened animal and lost 25 pounds. She experienced panic attacks and refused chemotherapy for breast cancer. Isolation and fear brought her to an understanding of her son's suicidal feelings. Frozen grief made her want to die.

While I intuitively sense the sticky nature of grief, Dr. Doka's concept of disenfranchised grief helps me cognitively grasp how and why Mother Hunger is so paralyzing. There is no place to talk about this injury and very little public awareness. Even the now widely respected ACE questionnaire fails to list "having an abusive or frightening mother" on the questionnaire. (It does include witnessing one's mother be abused, however, illustrating how we can make room for mothers as victims but not as perpetrators.) Disenfranchised grief is so intrinsically woven into the fabric of Mother Hunger that it's normal; *frozen grief is the essence of Mother Hunger.*

In the field of psychology, the concept of "normal" grief tells us that grieving happens in predictable stages that end with resolution.[5] "Abnormal" grief, however, according to psychology experts, doesn't move through predictable stages. It stays stuck in patterns of mourning. Patterns of mourning look like the following:

- **Protest**: Arguing or demanding, and angry outbursts.
- **Pining**: Prolonged mourning, being haunted by loss.
- **Despair**: Depression, hopeless, and resignation.

- **Disconnection**: Dissociation, frozen mourning. Sometimes an addictive process, behavior, or substance steps in and the mourning process doesn't happen at all.

Since each woman with Mother Hunger is lodged somewhere in the morass of "abnormal" grief—stuck in various patterns of protest, pining, despair, and disconnection— these symptoms aren't abnormal to me. In fact, these particular grief symptoms are so common that I give them a name. For example, an apology ache is part of the pining stage. Naming an apology ache helps women begin letting go of the fantasy that their mother might eventually say "I'm sorry." It also helps women avoid transferring the apology ache to a spouse, a friend, or a grown child.

Let Yourself Wallow

Living with Mother Hunger is like being trapped inside a cage of rage and longing. Like Sue Klebold, sometimes you can't eat. Sometimes you eat so much you feel sick. These patterns are *normal*. As you heal, the emotions you weren't allowed to feel as a little girl will be rising up. Sometimes grief will feel like anxiety or anger rather than sadness or despair. Allowing yourself to feel these emotions may seem wrong and disorienting because we are wired to avoid emotional pain. Plus, our culture expects us to brush off emotional adversity quickly, leaving us without time for grief.

In Tina Gilbertson's book *Constructive Wallowing*, she shares a powerful tool that works really well for healing Mother Hunger. She invites us to wallow—wallow in sadness, grief, and despair. I love how Gilbertson reworks wallowing, reframing the negative connotations of laziness or self-pity into an active, useful process. Gilbertson sees wallowing as "(w)allowing"—allowing emotions to have room and attention. While some might consider wallowing indulgent, I think Gilbertson is right on. Wallowing is a powerful way to move through difficult emotions. Pushing them down doesn't work; we just get depressed. Repressing them won't work; they leak out in other ways. Denial further abandons the little girl inside us who tucked away the emotions her mother couldn't tolerate. We already know how to do that. It's time to learn something new.

Wallowing may sound scary. You may wonder if negative emotions could overwhelm you. What if you never get out of bed? These are normal concerns, but remind yourself that avoiding negative feelings is actually avoiding yourself. Healing comes from facing your fear, from being present with the wounded parts of you that your mother didn't see and couldn't tolerate. Let disenfranchised feelings wash into your soul. Face the pieces of yourself that you've been hiding. Wallow.

Whenever possible, take time away from work, partners, or children and tend to these feelings. Cover yourself with a heavy blanket and curl up as if you were being embraced by a loving mother.

Belonging

Here's how one woman describes her healing:

Three years after my mom died was the first holiday that I did not hurt from her absence. . . . I celebrated my mom with some pics on social media and spent the day with my garden—Mother Nature has always held reverence for me and I treasure being her steward. I have mother cousins and mother-in-laws that are treasures to me and spent time being celebrated by my family with a beautiful meal.[6]

Finding places to belong heals Mother Hunger. Without a sense of belonging, we default to addictive substitutes to numb our loneliness. While loneliness might feel safer than risking connection, finding a place where you have temporary relief from your own thinking is an essential piece of healing Mother Hunger. Bruce Alexander's pioneering research on addiction makes this truth irrefutable. In his research, he noticed that when rats were placed alone in a cage with a bottle of regular water and a bottle of cocaine-infused water, they drank the cocaine water to the point of illness and death. However, when Alexander gave the little mammals something to do (toys, wheels) and some companions (other rats), the animals drank the regular water and avoided the cocaine water.[7] Since rats have brains similar to ours, Alexander's study highlights and normalizes our need for human belonging.

Finding a place to belong sounds much easier than it is. You have probably tried. Groups of women can be scary places. You might have learned that churches aren't safe either. For this reason, I love 12-step programs. They are free, nonjudgmental places to belong. If the idea terrifies you, try a phone meeting or an online group like InTheRooms or Seeking Integrity (www.seekingintegrity.com) for support.

Divorcing Mom

Sometimes, a mother's behavior and her lack of remorse is so painful that it requires you to separate from her. "Divorcing" Mom is a last resort that's not about a solution for Mother Hunger—it's more a survival strategy. You simply can't allow yourself to have continued exposure to her.

When you face this decision, be sure you make it with the consultation and care of a professional who witnesses your heartache. Deciding to divorce your mother should never be done in anger or as an attempt to "win" and finally feel powerful. Instead, like any other healthy boundary, a decision of this magnitude must come after careful consideration and from a place of peace. That's not to say you won't feel sad. Grief is part of any divorce process. And divorcing your mother can be the most painful divorce of all.

A Celestial Mother

When you're healing from a traumatic breakup or injury, you need someone to be there for you . . . someone you can rely on at 3 A.M. when things feel bleak, or first thing in the morning when the world feels heavy from the onset. In these moments, your heart seeks a maternal figure who knows and loves you, someone who isn't burdened by your fears. In such moments, some of my clients find it helpful to lean into the embrace of a celestial mother.

Historically, humans have revered and worshipped both feminine and masculine deities. In fact, many recognize the Judeo-Christian god of the Bible as being both male and female. However, patriarchal forces have sought to erase the feminine side of god from the collective psyche. For this reason, you might need help creating a celestial mother. Your resourcefulness will come into play here. Let your imagination assist you. If you're not feeling particularly imaginative, consider the effort it took to create a fantasy mother as a little girl. You can do this.

Let yourself dream. What would your ideal mother be like? (If your mother is still alive, you may hang on to the hope that she will change instead of doing the imaginative work that this requires. But by now you already know this is a delay tactic, a way to avoid grief.) If you have no idea how to create an ideal mother, you could explore the goddess figures we have historically worshipped. For a nurturing mother, think of the Greek goddess Gaia. Maternal soul of the earth, Gaia provides life and nourishment. Sometimes known as Mother Earth, Gaia has a name in each culture. If you need a protective mother, Kali is a powerful goddess to call on. Kali is the Hindu goddess who destroys evil forces and preserves freedom. Widely worshipped in India, Kali is the divine protector. Imagine what she might do to help you. Who would she fight? Where would she take you for safety? For guidance, you might study the goddesses who balance fierceness with wisdom, like Athena and Persephone. How do they make difficult choices?

There are other places to look for inspiration also. Are there women in your life who you find attractive? If so, what draws you to them? Is it their warmth, strength, confidence, or beauty? If you can't think of anyone personally, what about a character from a book or movie who inspires you? Maybe it's Wonder Woman, with her superhuman powers, bracelets that stop bullets, and a magic lasso that makes people tell the truth. Inspired by love, the creator of Wonder Woman was William Marston. His mistress, Olive, happened to be the daughter of Ethel Byrne, who along with her sister Margaret Sanger developed what is now Planned Parenthood and provided some of the earliest access to birth control.[8] There is a lot to this story if you need inspiration.

The point here is to allow yourself permission to turn inward with a deliberate purpose: to find a celestial mother who can offer you kindness and love. Then lean into that love. As you do, love will weave its way into your tissues, and in time, you may become your own inner mother, filled with a well of tenderness and protection.

EMDR

For those of you already working with a therapist, you might know about EMDR (eye movement desensitization and reprocessing). Maybe you tried it. If so, I hope you found it helpful, but if it didn't work for you, perhaps it's because you couldn't find a "safe place." "Safe place" is part of the original protocol designed by Francine Shapiro. While "safe place" is a proven strategy for beginning EMDR, it can be a roadblock for those of you who have no idea what a safe place actually feels like.

A few years ago, using EMDR to help a client imprint her celestial mother, I found the standard EMDR protocol "safe place" blocked the process. In fact, again and again, this happened. Many of my clients simply couldn't find a "safe place." Women without maternal protection often don't know the sensation of safety. Asking them to find a "safe place" seemed to cause unnecessary frustration or shame. Avoidant clients got annoyed and decided to skip EMDR. More anxious clients tried it to please me, but the protocol was stale and cold. After a few failures, I was frustrated too. I decided to see if EMDR could work without a "safe place." It did work. And the benefits were too good to ignore. Quietly, I was getting great results.

Attending the 2017 EMDR International Association conference, the work of Marshall Wilensky, Ph.D., and Katie O'Shea, M.S., caught my attention. Their working paper titled "When Safe Place Doesn't Work" literally stopped me in my tracks. Reading their paper validated my experience with "safe place" and also educated me about a small window of time in utero before a fetus is connected to the biological mother. During the first five to six weeks post conception, the primitive nervous system is in place (we have a brain at the end of four weeks), and there are about 100,000 neurons firing, so it's possible that some of the experience before we were attached to our biological mothers is stored in our body and mind. Perhaps, they suggest, in that tiny window, before attaching to an anxious, ambivalent, or unhappy mother, there might be a body memory of safety.

Feeling better, I unapologetically modified EMDR with clients with a renewed confidence that the internal sensation of safety might exist. Fast-forward another year and I meet Dr. Laurel Parnell, mother of Attachment-Focused EMDR. She validated the reasons why the counting protocol that is also part of traditional EMDR wasn't working so well for me or my clients. Helpful guidance like this is so, well, helpful. Hopefully, if you gave up on EMDR previously, you might consider trying it again with a clinician who has trained with Dr. Laurel Parnell.

Long-Term Relational Trauma

When the body has been a battleground, disorganized attachment patterns are enduring. Earning security requires more effort than healing milder forms of Mother Hunger. If you are a victim of Third-Degree Mother Hunger, first and foremost you need to find a safe relationship with someone invested in your well-being. Patricia DeYoung writes that "long-term relational trauma leaves our psyches indelibly marked."[9] Third-Degree Mother Hunger is a long-term relational trauma. The "indelible" mark is scar tissue on your heart. This is why you need a competent guide to help you. Trauma from Third-Degree Mother Hunger won't heal without a safe relationship. The lack of this relationship explains why women don't get better in residential inpatient hospitals.

Fundamentally, the treatment for this unspeakable wound must focus first on the disorganized attachment rather than the trauma, because the broken maternal relationship *is* the trauma. A safe relationship with one trustworthy adult *is* the cure. Once a safe relationship is established, trauma work might not even be necessary, because attachment healing *is* trauma healing.

This sophisticated attachment healing process requires a trauma-informed therapist—someone who can safely get lost *with* you in the disorientation and disorganization that you feel in your mind and body; someone who can tolerate the depth of grief you're experiencing. Only when you feel *felt*—when your body knows that someone is deeply experiencing this madness with you—can you come home to yourself.

Out of the Storm (www.outofthestorm.website) is a helpful resource for finding a trauma-informed therapist

Closure

Inside each woman who seeks support for Mother Hunger is a baby girl whose language I get to learn. My clients don't care what car I drive, where I live, or whether or not I eat gluten (well, initially, some of them do). As we settle into treatment, they mostly need me to be fully present, to notice each micromovement in their face and respond accordingly. I don't always get it right. But when I miss a cue and there's a momentary disconnection, it's a chance for repair—a chance to model what it looks like when a caring woman takes responsibility for the well-being of the relationship. This is good therapy in action. And this is what a trauma-informed therapist provides.

Healing Mother Hunger is a nonlinear, fluid process. No timeline can reveal the necessary effort or schedule that will yield the best results. However, what I have found very helpful is to let go of the idea of a finish line. You don't need this pressure. Like an apology ache, seeking closure is longing for a fantasy. Even when you use all the tools and your life starts looking up, there will be days when grief finds you again—like on Mother's Day. Mother's Day is a particularly dreadful day for so many adult daughters. Below is an e-mail I received that captures the feelings that many women experience:

Hi Kelly,
Thank you for the invitation to write to you. I hate Mother's Day. My own mother was insatiable regarding cards, gifts, and phone calls, and none were good enough for her. This day was a setup for failure each year and I dreaded it. I became a step-mom in my 30s and then this day was doubly awful since the three kids were off with their dad, or all of us would go to buy presents and cards for their mom. I felt [like] an imposter and a fake trying to participate while thinking, "This is not my job."

I don't have children of my own and each year I need to prepare that my stepchildren may or may not text or call. It is a lonely day. If I go out and grocery clerks, restaurant personnel, [or] shop owners wish me a happy Mother's Day, I respectfully smile, but inside I feel like a fraud. My own mother once said, "Having stepchildren, that's not really being a mother, is it?" This year completely caught me by surprise and with the virus it was extra hard. Next year I will be better prepared.

When grief creeps back in, it can be discouraging. You may think it's a sign you aren't healing. But this isn't true. The ongoing grief that is part of Mother Hunger is connected to what's known as *ambiguous loss*. It's difficult to face a problem without a promise of a quick, pain-free solution. The lack of tidy closure, however, is the nature of disenfranchised grief and ambiguous loss, not an indication of pathology.

Rather than expecting your heart to be free of periodic achiness, notice the moments when you no longer hide under a blanket of shame. While this wound may never feel fully healed, you will gain an inner peace as you replace lost maternal care and transform pain into purpose. In this way, you will become more able to tolerate the inevitable dark days. I find Patricia DeYoung's work with toxic shame helpful as it relates to healing. She says that we can become shame resilient. "Shame can be transformed. And the transformation happens in connection with someone who is close and regulates our nervous system."[10]

The same holds true for Mother Hunger.

As you work to replace lost nurturance, protection, and guidance, remember that this is an ongoing process. You're building a new brain, and like any new routine, it takes time before you feel the results. Please don't do all this by yourself. You've been alone long enough. Your body is designed for well-being, but we are relational creatures and we need connection with others. Healing Mother Hunger brings you home—home to yourself—but it's really helpful when you have a village around your home.

Reclaiming Damaged Dreams and Goals

This is a fun and fruitful way to identify your desires and dreams. To start, let's prime your brain.

Think of four of your significant achievements to date. What are you most proud of accomplishing? (For example, abstaining from alcohol or completing an academic program or moving to a new town are all significant achievements.)

-
-
-
-

What are four ways you express creativity? (Planning meals, entertaining friends and family, or creating music and art are just a few ideas.)

-
-
-
-

What gives your life meaning? List four things that get you out of bed in the morning. (Try to think of things that make you smile, like your pet, yoga class, or cup of coffee.)

-
-
-
-

Now your brain is ready for the next part.

Think of seven words to describe yourself, such as *funny, pretty, resilient, creative.* (This is the "self" that feels most like you, not the "self" that worries about what others think.)

-
-
-
-
-
-

Think of seven things that you like to do and that give you a sense of purpose and meaning. (Go back to the first three lists if you need ideas.)

-
-
-
-
-
-
-

When you have all fourteen, pick your top three descriptive words. (For example, words to describe yourself might include *strong, pretty, persistent, funny, quiet*, and *intelligent*. But now you pick your favorite three, such as (1) *funny*, (2) *persistent*, (3) *pretty*.)

-
-
-

Now pick your favorite three activities. (For example, (1) *reading*, (2) *cooking*, (3) *knitting*.)

-
-
-

Now it's time for the finale: let's operationalize what you have put together. Taking your top three from each category, make a sentence. (For example, *I am funny, persistent, and pretty so that I can read, cook, and knit.*)

When you have your sentence, think of this as your internal compass for life. This can provide guidance for your choices and decisions.

How much of your day-to-day reflects this statement? 10 percent? 30 percent? 60 percent?

What can you do to increase the percentage?

The more your life reflects who you really are, the less you need to fill the emptiness with unhealthy behaviors or people.

CHAPTER 10

MOTHERING WITH MOTHER HUNGER

I love working with mothers in all life stages, because together, we stop the generational transmission of Mother Hunger. If you are reading this and feeling regret because your children are grown, take comfort in knowing that your healing positively impacts them—at any age. This is not because you tell your adult children about what you're doing; in fact, they most likely don't want or need to hear about it. It's because as you are healing, the way you speak, your facial expressions, even the way your body moves, change. Energetically, your body sends messages of safety and comfort to everyone around you. Replacing lost elements of maternal love improves how you love yourself and others.

I've found that women who heal the pain of Mother Hunger become very attentive, loving mothers. Time and again, I've witnessed the transformation of fractured bonds between adult daughters and their mothers. As I stated earlier, since we never truly outgrow the desire for a mother, daughters most always appreciate their mother's repair efforts. For those of you who already have children, be encouraged; as you heal from Mother Hunger, your efforts transfer to your children.

Beginning with Babies

If you are considering mothering a child, this note is for you. In truth, a deep exploration of mothering with Mother Hunger deserves a separate book. But for now, this short section may help.

I'd like to emphasize that each element your little one needs—nurturance, protection, and guidance—you need, too. To nurture well, you need nurturing from friends and family. To protect your baby, you must be safe. Since you may desire different things for your baby than your mother gave you, you need guidance from other mothers. Women who support your desire to attach to your baby. Mothers who applaud your desire to be gentle and responsive. Mothers who have navigated this journey themselves.

Rest assured, even with Mother Hunger, you can nurture well when you let Mother Nature be your guide. I will share some helpful ideas to buffer culturally dominant but misguided information about infant care so you have more options for important choices.

It can be healing, even freeing to discover guidance that isn't toxic or agenda driven. Recently, a client shared with me an exciting resource for women who are ambivalent about having children: "motherhood clarity coaching." This type of coaching helps women wade through cultural pressures and generational expectations to find their own truth about whether or not motherhood is the best option for them. Having children is life-changing and is certainly not for everyone. Having support for this big decision is critical, as pressure comes from many directions, making it all the more difficult.

Frequently, Mother Hunger alters your body-based guidance system for nurturing a baby. Particularly for those of you with Third-Degree Mother Hunger, the feeling of pure love for your baby or child can be so foreign that it brings anxiety and dissociative states along with the compelling desire to nurture and protect. These polarizing emotions can be terribly confusing and can overwhelm the bonding and attachment process. It helps to anticipate this and know that it's normal.

Psychotherapist Susan Forward, Ph.D., says, "There's no magic switch that turns on maternal instinct and ensures that a woman, especially a troubled one, will suddenly bond with her baby."[1] While there is an element of truth here, particularly if you have Third-Degree Mother Hunger, you *do* have a magic switch—oxytocin. Nature gives you what you need to bond with your baby. Unfortunately, our culture doesn't support nature in this powerful attachment process. Demands from the outside world put incredible pressure on you. Problems arise when misinformed experts get involved and redirect nature's way of helping you become a mother. Be cautious of sleep training experts who tell you that your baby can self-soothe, that your baby needs separation, or that your toddler needs a time out; these folks are not concerned with attachment. Their poor advice can keep you from accessing nature's magic switch and developing the nurturing behavior you and your baby need.

Oxytocin: Nature's Magic Switch

Like every other mammal, we are biologically wired to bond with our babies. Biology delivers powerful neurochemical support to help us become mothers. Recall the last time you felt deeply connected to someone. Did you feel warm? Hopeful?

Bonding is enjoyable because oxytocin is at work, creating a positive experience that you will want again and again—not because you're needy, but because you're human. Oxytocin, sometimes called the *love hormone*, is a powerful neurotransmitter that floods the body when you cuddle with someone you love, experience an orgasm, give birth, or make breast milk. Both men and women have oxytocin receptors that facilitate bonding. Women have more opportunity to experience oxytocin if we give birth or breastfeed, but even without either experience, proximity, holding, cuddling, and caring for a child beckons oxytocin.

Oxytocin transforms an adult into a parent—turning you from a maiden into a mother. Becoming responsible for the well-being of a vulnerable, completely dependent little human is an incredible undertaking, and you will change. Change hurts. Even if we want it, we may resist it. Resisting this particular opportunity for change only makes mothering harder. Embrace the opportunity to pause, slow down, be curious, and tune in to the changes in yourself and the needs of your child.

If you were nursed and cuddled a lot as a child, adapting to this new chapter will come more easily for you than if you were not properly nurtured. Without an inner sense of what it feels like to be cared for in a sensitive, tuned-in kind of way, caring for a baby or toddler can feel both unnatural and terrifying. In this case, knowing that biology is on your side helps. Allow Mother Nature to guide you by listening to your baby's cues for comfort, food, and closeness.

Hold your baby as much as you can so you turn on the maternal magic switch. The flow of oxytocin depends on this. There is no need to worry about creating an overly dependent baby. Babies cannot be spoiled. A baby who is touched a lot grows a bigger, better brain. A mother who stays close to her infant grows a maternal heart. Oxytocin and prolactin (a milk-making hormone) are designed to slow you down so you can bond with your baby. The hazy "mommy brain" that you've heard about or might be feeling right now is purposeful lethargy; it is nature's invitation to relax and be with your newborn. Refer to Chapter 3: Nurturance for more information about these powerful hormones.

Epigenetic Inheritance

Toxic stress, generations of sexual objectification, lack of support, and unaddressed Mother Hunger leave many mothers without the epigenetic wisdom to guide their passage from maiden to mother. As most epigenetic transmission goes through the matrilineal line, your mother's story impacts your own. She could only give what she received. The science of epigenetics informs us that we inherit the resilience and trauma of our ancestors.

New mothers need the same care that a baby does: nurturance, protection, and guidance. In some ways, those of you with Mother Hunger are as vulnerable as your newborn, because you don't have the maternal support you need as you make this powerful transition. To stop the transmission of Mother Hunger, surround yourself with a team who will feed you and protect you while you take the necessary time to bond with your newborn. Early nurturance and safety in the first three years is the best insurance against adversity and stress. (Hiring a postpartum doula is a great start for you and your newborn.)

Childbirth and Stress

Many women in North America haven't witnessed childbirth before they face it, so the natural process of birth can be strange and frightening. If you are preparing for childbirth, an understanding of your amazing female body helps build your confidence before your baby even arrives. Knowledge is power.

Nature's first effort to help you become a mother begins as oxytocin rushes in to buffer childbirth pain. During labor, as contractions build, so does oxytocin. Oxytocin diminishes your modesty at the same time, helping you settle into the rhythm of labor.

Unfortunately, biology hasn't developed an oxytocin formula strong enough to combat the frightening sounds, noxious smells, and disturbing lights in hospitals. Fear complicates childbirth, prompting a neural cascade of adrenaline and cortisol that is very unhelpful during labor. These hormones are necessary for fighting or fleeing but counterproductive during childbirth.

Women aren't meant to labor in these sterile and chaotic conditions. Research shows that we fare better in familiar surroundings, with dim lights and soft sounds, while giving birth. We also need the presence of other women—women who are calm and confident and caring. For this reason, I hope you consider hospital alternatives, such as a birthing center, a midwife, and/or a doula. The increasing popularity of doulas is an encouraging trend. Doulas are companions who comfort, encourage, and aid you during and after labor. Doulas work alongside medical providers and midwives, but their sole purpose is to support the mother. Research shows that having a doula present enhances your oxytocin release.[2] With a doula by your side, birth is less frightening and you have a better chance for early bonding with your baby.

Nursing

Human milk is designed specifically for a new little human. Your breast milk protects your baby from disease while the immune system is young. Breast milk regulates metabolism and promotes rapid brain growth for your newborn. Suckling frequently calms your baby and relaxes you. Mother's milk is the perfect formula (no pun intended) for bonding and attachment. If you are adopting a baby, you might want to explore the ways you can stimulate lactation or consider purchasing human milk from a milk bank.

As I mentioned earlier, I prefer the term *nursing* to *breast-feeding*, because nursing happens with a bottle or a breast. And it is not just feeding. Nursing is holding, cuddling, singing, cleaning, and tending. Nursing is nurturance.

While the advantages of breast milk are well known, most doctors are not adequately trained to support you with this amazing process. So here are some helpful things to know if you wish to nurse your baby:

- Most infants are not very hungry the first 48 to 72 hours, so their sucking reflex might not be strong enough to latch on correctly.

- It's normal that you might experience plugged milk ducts and soreness as milk comes in. When this happens, it hurts. Have a plan from a midwife, a doula, an IBCLC certified lactation consultant, or a La Leche League volunteer ahead of time.

- Prolactin, the hormone that prompts your body to make milk, relies on supply and demand. Skin contact and frequent suckling boosts prolactin. The more stimulation to nipple and skin, the more milk flow.

- Nursing often and for long periods of time boosts your relaxation and gives your baby the best chance for reaching hindmilk—the creamy, rich part of your breast milk that comes later in the feeding session and stimulates infant brain growth.

- Centuries of genetic coding wire your baby for closeness with your body. At birth, your baby can already smell your milk and knows your scent. Closeness with your baby is the best thing for your milk supply and for creating secure attachment.

The vulnerability of a body that's sore from birth and suddenly making milk can be overwhelming. Breastfeeding takes time to learn. Just because it's biological doesn't mean it's entirely intuitive. You are beginning a new relationship, and like any new relationship, it's amazing, awkward, exhilarating, confusing, and sometimes painful. If it becomes too stressful to nurse your baby from your breast, be assured that your little one can thrive with your sensitive care regardless of how you feed her. Bottle feeding is a salvation for mothers and a cuddly time for babies when eye contact and physical touch are part of the ritual. Fortunately, even when feeding from your breast isn't going well, skin-to-skin contact, shared cuddling, and playful interactions will keep your oxytocin flowing.

If you take away only one thing from this note, I encourage you to reach out to lactation specialists, doulas, or La Leche League volunteers before your baby arrives. Building a support team gives you the best chance for success in the early months together. I want you to have lots of support, because if you have Mother Hunger, the hormonal benefits that come with nursing are very important for helping you transition from being a busy adult to being a soothing parent. As a new mother, you need as much nurturance as your newborn does. Whether you give birth or adopt, this is the most vulnerable time in your life after your own infancy. Your best guidance comes from tuning in to your baby's cues. But this can be challenging in a world that demands your attention in many directions.

Rather than feeding schedules designed by formula companies, or advice from sleep training experts, listen to your baby. Your baby knows what he or she needs to feel secure. What works for one baby won't for another. Some babies are harder to soothe than others due to exposure to maternal distress in utero. Interrupted breastfeeding rhythms can cause early feeding problems that complicate bonding. Prolactin slows down without adequate nipple stimulation, diminishing milk production. You may struggle with sadness or shame if breastfeeding is difficult or when your baby cries. If you are stressed, you may avoid holding your baby, which will diminish your oxytocin levels. It's easy to get caught in a paralyzing cycle of anxiety and depression when this happens. These challenges are normal. If you aren't making enough milk for your baby, it's likely you need more support and guidance. Perhaps no one has told you that nursing a baby is a full-time job, or that nighttime closeness with your baby boosts your milk supply for daytime hours when you might be away. This is why sleep training, which some professionals suggest should begin as early as possible, is terrible for milk production and stressful for bonding.

Breaking the Cycle of Mother Hunger

You may be disoriented or shocked by the reality of motherhood. The loss of freedom, the absence of control, and the huge responsibility can be overwhelming. Carrying the burden of Mother Hunger complicates these normal feelings. The mix of pure joy and abject terror can initiate an emotional crisis. Loving your baby wakes the buried truth inside your heart and touches your own deprivation and heartache. The intensity of these emotions can be too much to manage without your own mother's support. I hope that when this happens, you have safe surroundings and helpful relationships to comfort and protect you.

I'm so glad you're here learning about nature's design and how important it is for you to have the nurturance, protection, and guidance that your child also needs. With awareness, tenderness, and preparation, you can mother yourself *while* nurturing your baby. In fact, becoming a mother may be the first time you care for yourself, because life is no longer just about you, and caring for yourself is also what's best for your child. As you nurture yourself with good food, sleep, and connection with other women, you stop the intergenerational transmission of Mother Hunger. At any stage of mothering, your healing is a gift to your child—and to the world.

Resources for Mothering

- The Baby-Friendly Hospital Initiative (BFHI), launched in 1991, is an effort to ensure that all maternity facilities, whether freestanding or in a hospital, become centers of breastfeeding support. Their website can guide you to a supportive facility in your area.

- Attachment Parenting International supports parents with science-based, attachment-focused advice. Their newsletter is very helpful.

- Darcia Narvaez is a researcher whose work focuses on "lifelong human wellness" and "meeting the biological needs of infants."[3] I recommend her book *Neurobiology and the Development of Human Morality: Evolution, Culture, and Wisdom* and her blog (evolvednest.org).

- *The Baby Book: Everything You Need to Know About Your Baby from Birth to Age Two,* by William and Martha Sears, is an excellent guide from a doctor and a nurse who have raised children and now have grandchildren.

- *The Attachment Parenting Book: A Commonsense Guide to Understanding and Nurturing Your Baby* is another excellent resource from the Sears Parenting Library.

- *Nighttime Parenting: How to Get Your Baby and Child to Sleep*, by William Sears, explains how parenting at night is just as critical as parenting during the day.

- Raised Good: This blog is full of supportive guidance for natural parenting in the modern world and offers online courses (https://raisedgood.com).

CONCLUSION

Stress makes us irritable. Our face gets tight, we don't smile, and our voice sounds harsh or brittle. As I finish this manuscript through the perils of COVID-19, vulnerable mothers and children are heavy on my mind, because I know that the stress is simply too much for them. This book would not be possible if I were still mothering daily. It demanded that I find the right language for how primitive heartbreak happens, to find descriptions for the various ways mothers fail their little ones—loving mothers, good mothers, and dedicated mothers; mothers who wanted children, who felt ready, and who did their very best; mothers like me, who were unable to offer what they simply didn't have. I couldn't have done it if I were mothering in a pandemic.

Pandemic aside, writing about Mother Hunger is one of the hardest things I've ever done. Even if I were writing something yummy, like a cookbook, I would have struggled. Writing is just difficult. Luckily, in the early stages of preparation, I found the book *Eleanor Oliphant Is Completely Fine* by Gail Honeyman. Reading her brilliant portrayal of a deprived, dissociated daughter was the perfect companion for writing about Mother Hunger. Honeyman's leading lady is the poster child for Mother Hunger, experiencing the burning need to numb out with fantasy and the split self that emerges from early heartbreak.

Spoiler alert: Honeyman writes a fictional character as real as my clinical cases. In the story, Eleanor Oliphant manufactures a love affair with a man she has never met. It's one of the most compelling stories of love addiction I've seen. She also has weekly phone calls with her cruel, critical mother. This might be reasonable, except that her mother is dead. Her manufactured phone calls illustrate one way a daughter survives unbearable grief and trauma. Oliphant's vodka-infused isolation almost leaves her homeless and represents every woman's worst nightmare. Oliphant, who never knew a mother's love, shares a powerful truth: "loneliness is the new cancer."

During this pandemic, as we cover our faces, masking our smiles from each other, I can't help but think of the implications of isolation from COVID-19. Recently, a photographer who takes pictures of babies and toddlers told me she's noticed that in the past four months, it's been increasingly difficult to get babies to smile. Her observation has me thinking of Beatrice Beebe's research and pondering the long-term impact of infants gazing into masked faces. What are their mirror neurons losing?

While masks are discouraging, other stories of babies and their caregivers in quarantine together are hopeful. Little ones born in 2020 enter a world that keeps Mom and other caregivers close. Daily, I hear from parents about how they are finding gifts in the shared quarantine with their babies. They are taking turns with infant care, toddler care, domestic duties, and career responsibilities. This is not without stress. No one is immune from the stress of the pandemic. But for little ones, the benefit of consistent adult proximity might have rewards.

Domestic violence and financial insecurity erode the benefits of proximity, however, and the staggering numbers of families living with chronic fear have terrible implications for Third-Degree Mother Hunger. Physicians report concern about children in violent situations. California invested $42 million to protect children who are at heightened risk of abuse and mistreatment due to COVID-19.[1] Perhaps the good news is that COVID-19 is bringing increased awareness of ACEs and the impact of toxic stress on children.[2] Organizations like ACEs Connection, the Robert Wood Johnson Foundation, and Iowa ACEs 360, to name a few, are invested in research and activism to support children and families.

In a recent CBS *Sunday Morning* episode during COVID-19, I was encouraged to find an entire segment about the benefits of oxytocin. The report encouraged us to hug ourselves.[3] And a few weeks later on the same program, there was a feature on smiling and mirroring.[4] *Scientific American* published an article by Lydia Denworth, author of *Friendship*, titled "The Loneliness of the 'Social Distancer' Triggers Brain Cravings Akin to Hunger."[5] Educational reports like these remove the shame attached to loneliness, because we know we are all feeling it. The pandemic is forcing loneliness out of the closet and demanding that we pay attention to our need for one another. Going forward, I hope we hold on to this information.

We don't know exactly how the social isolation, school closures, and economic disruption caused by COVID-19 will affect our mental health, but we know it will. Divorce rates are rising. Mothers are suffering as they juggle the impossible, conflicting demands of work and home. Stress has our biological alarm system in overdrive. In the best scenario, we will emerge with greater respect for those who tend and befriend under duress, because more than ever, we need someone to keep the house sanitary, food in the pantry, and family members close. Generally, these duties fall to women, but occasionally gender roles are dissolving under the shared pressure of a long-term pandemic. Couples and families work together, because if everyone were fighting or fleeing, relationships would simply fall apart. Respecting the instinct to tend and befriend has lasting implications for our humanitarian responses to one another.

There is no way to accurately predict what the world will look like when this book arrives in your hands. Will we be a stronger, more compassionate community? Will we have a new awareness and respect for infants' needs and our own? Will the tend-and-befriend response have us taking better care of one another? Or will we adapt to new levels of isolation using food, alcohol, or whatever mood-altering thing we can find?

I take solace, and perhaps you can too, from Margaret Renkl's *Late Migrations*. Her beautiful words have a prophetic nature as she says, "There is nothing to fear. There is nothing at all to fear. Walk out into the springtime, and look: the birds welcome you with a chorus. The flowers turn their faces to your face. The last of last year's leaves, still damp in the shadows, smell ripe and faintly of fall."[6] Her memoir speaks to the enduring nature of Mother Nature, who is here for us.

Solace for Mother Hunger is in the natural world. Nurture and protect her so she can nurture and protect *you*. Plant things, tidy your closet, eat food that nourishes your spirit. Tend to your heartache and befriend those who understand your journey. As you heal, rest when you are tired and afraid until you remember "there is nothing to fear."

ENDNOTES

Introduction

1. Lisa Donovan, *Our Lady of Perpetual Hunger: A Memoir* (New York: Penguin Press, 2020), 83.

Chapter 1

1. Erica Komisar, *Being There: Why Prioritizing Motherhood in the First Three Years Matters* (New York: TarcherPerigee, 2017), 36.

2. Marcy Axness, *Parenting for Peace: Raising the Next Generation of Peacemakers* (Boulder, CO: Sentient, 2012), 192.

3. Gabor Maté, *In the Realm of Hungry Ghosts: Close Encounters with Addiction* (Berkeley, CA: North Atlantic Books, 2010), 436, as cited in Axness, *Parenting for Peace*, 193.

4. Axness, *Parenting for Peace*, 194.

5. Komisar, *Being There*, 36.

6. Amir Levine and Rachel Heller, *Attached: The New Science of Adult Attachment and How It Can Help You Find—And Keep—Love* (New York: TarcherPerigree, 2010).

7. Maia Szalavitz and Bruce D. Perry, *Born for Love: Why Empathy Is Essential—and Endangered* (New York: William Morrow, 2011), 20.

8. Gwen Dewar, "Newborn Cognitive Development: What Do Babies Know, and How Do They Learn?," Parenting Science, accessed December 2, 2020, https://www.parentingscience.com/newborn-cognitive-development.html.

9. Daniel J. Siegel and Tina Payne Bryson, *The Whole-Brain Child: 12 Revolutionary Strategies to Nurture Your Child's Developing Mind* (New York: Bantam, 2012).

10. Maureen M. Black et al., "Early Childhood Development Coming of Age: Science Through the Life Course," *Lancet* 389, no. 10064 (2017): 77–90.

11. Erin P. Hambrick et al., "Beyond the ACE Score: Examining Relationships Between Timing of Developmental Adversity, Relational Health and Developmental Outcomes in Children," *Archives of Psychiatric Nursing* 33, no. 3 (2019): 238–247.

12. Allan Schore, "The American Bowlby: An Interview with Allan Schore," telephone interview by Roz Carroll in March 2001.

13. Centers for Disease Control and Prevention, "Essentials for Childhood: Creating Safe, Stable, Nurturing Relationships and Environments for All Children," accessed November 18, 2020, https://www.cdc.gov/violenceprevention/pdf/essentials-for-childhood-framework508.pdf.

14. Megan H. Bair-Merritt et al., "A Framework for Thriving: A Comprehensive Approach to Child Health—CHCS Blog," Center for Health Care Strategies, October 13, 2020, https://www.chcs.org/a-framework-for-thriving-a-comprehensive-approach-to-child-health.

15. Komisar, *Being There*, 207.

16. Jhoanna Robledo, "Developmental Milestone: Separation and Independence," BabyCenter, December 12, 2018, https://www.babycenter.com/baby/baby-development/developmental-milestone-separation-and-independence_6577.

17. Harvard University Center on the Developing Child, "ACEs and Toxic Stress: Frequently Asked Questions," accessed September 20, 2020, https://developingchild.harvard.edu/resources/aces-and-toxic-stress-frequently-asked-questions; Adrienne Rich, "It Is Hard to Write About My Own Mother: On the Deep Complexity of the Mother–Daughter Relationship," Literary Hub, August 24, 2018, https://lithub.com/adrienne-rich-it-is-hard-to-write-about-my-own-mother.

18. Rich, "It is Hard to Write About My Own Mother."

19. Ibid.

20. Adrienne Rich, *Of Woman Born: Motherhood as Experience and Institution* (New York: W. W. Norton, 1986), 237.

21. Resmaa Menakem, *My Grandmother's Hands: Racialized Trauma and the Pathway to Mending Our Hearts and Bodies* (Las Vegas: Central Recovery Press, 2017), 42.

22. Donald Woods Winnicott, *Playing and Reality* (London: Tavistock, 1971).

23. Marco Iacoboni, "The Mirror Neuron Revolution: Explaining What Makes Humans Social," interview by Jonah Lehrer, *Scientific American,* July 1, 2008, https://www.scientificamerican.com/article/the-mirror-neuron-revolut.

24. "Why Former U.S. Surgeon General Vivek Murthy Believes Lone-liness Is a 'Profound' Public Health Issue," Washington Post Live video, 5:46, May 15, 2018, https://www.washingtonpost.com/video/postlive/former-surgeon-general-dr-vivek-murthy-people-who-are-lonely-live-shorter-lives/2018/05/15/4632188e-5853-11e8-9889-07bcc1327f4b_video.html.

Chapter 2

1. Daniel J. Siegel, "The Verdict Is In: The Case for Attachment Theory," *Psychotherapy Networker*, March/April 2011, https://www.psychotherapynetworker.org/magazine/article/343/the-verdict-is-in.

2. Daniel J. Siegel, *The Developing Mind: How Relationships and the Brain Interact to Shape Who We Are*, 2nd ed. (New York: Guilford, 2012), 91.

3. Psychology Hub, "Bowlby's Theory of Maternal Deprivation: Romanian Orphan Studies—Effects of Institutionalization," March 16, 2017, https://psychologyhub.co.uk/bowlbys-theory-of-maternal-deprivation-romanian-orphan-studies-effects-of-institutionalisation.

4. Kendra Cherry, "Biography of Psychologist John Bowlby: The Found-er of Attachment Theory," Verywell Mind, March 29, 2020, https://www.verywellmind.com/john-bowlby-biography-1907-1990-2795514.

5. Allan N. Schore, "Attachment and the Regulation of the Right Brain," *Attachment & Human Development* 2, no. 1 (2000): 23–47.

6. Allan N. Schore, "The Experience-Dependent Maturation of a Reg-ulatory System in the Orbital Prefrontal Cortex and the Origin of Developmental Psychopathology," *Development and Psychopathology* 8, no. 1 (Winter 1996): 59–87.

7. Peter Graf and Daniel L. Schacter, "Selective Effects of Interference on Implicit and Explicit Memory for New Associations," *Journal of Experimental Psychology: Learning, Memory, and Cognition* 13, no. 1 (1987): 45–53.

8. Brigid Schulte, "Effects of Child Abuse Can Last a Lifetime: Watch the 'Still Face' Experiment to See Why," *Washington Post* (blog), September 16, 2013, https://www.washingtonpost.com/blogs/she-the-people/wp/2013/09/16/affects-of-child-abuse-can-last-a-life-time-watch-the-still-face-experiment-to-see-why.

9. Schore, "Attachment and the Regulation of the Right Brain."

10. "Mother–Infant Communication: The Research of Dr. Beatrice Beebe Promo," produced by Karen Dougherty, YouTube video, 1:03, June 23, 2016, https://www.youtube.com/watch?v=rEMge2FeREw.

11. Levine and Heller, *Attached*.

12. Daniel P. Brown and David S. Elliott, *Attachment Disturbances in Adults: Treatment for Comprehensive Repair* (New York: W. W. Norton, 2016).

13. Jean Baker Miller, "Connections, Disconnections, and Violations," *Work in Progress* 33 (Wellesley, MA: Stone Center Working Paper Series, 1988): 5.

14. Sarah Peyton, "Are You Suffering from Alarmed Aloneness?," interview by *Om Times* podcast, July 12, 2019, http://podcast.omtimes.com/e/sarah-peyton-are-you-suffering-from-alarmed-aloneness.

Chapter 3

1. *South Africa Mail & Guardian*, "Your First 1000 Days Shape the Rest of Your Life," December 9, 2016, https://mg.co.za/article/2016-12-09-00-your-first-1000-days-shape-the-rest-of-your-life.

2. Dana G. Smith, "Opioid-Dependent Newborns Get New Treatment: Mom Instead of Morphine," California Health Care Foundation, August 1, 2019, https://www.chcf.org/blog/opioid-dependent-newborns-get-new-treatment.

3. Ashley M. Weber, Tondi M. Harrison, and Deborah K. Steward, "Expanding Regulation Theory with Oxytocin: A Psychoneurobiological Model for Infant Development," *Nursing Research* 67, no. 2 (March/April 2018): 133.

4. Elsevier, "Maternal Separation Stresses the Baby, Research Finds," ScienceDaily, November 2, 2011, https://www.sciencedaily.com/releases/2011/11/111102124955.htm.

5. Adrienne Santos-Longhurst, "Why Is Oxytocin Known as the 'Love Hormone'? And 11 Other FAQs," Healthline Parenthood, August 30, 2018, https://www.healthline.com/health/love-hormone.

6. Jill Bergman, "Skin-to-Skin Contact," La Leche League International, November 8, 2018, https://www.llli.org/skin-to-skin-contact; Darcia Narvaez, "The Tremendous Benefits of Breast Milk: An Evolved Nest Podcast," Kindred Media, August 6, 2020, https://www.kindredmedia.org/2020/08/the-tremendous-benefits-of-breast-milk-an-evolved-nest-podcast.

7. Michael J. Meaney, "Maternal Care, Gene Expression, and the Transmission of Individual Differences in Stress Reactivity Across Generations," *Annual Review of Neuroscience* 24, no. 1 (2001): 1170.

8. Linda Richter, *The Importance of Caregiver-Child Interactions for the Survival and Healthy Development of Young Children: A Review* (Geneva,

Switzerland: World Health Organization, 2004), https://www.who.
int/maternal_child_adolescent/documents/924159134X/en.

9. Ibid.

10. Harry F. Harlow, Margaret Kuenne Harlow, and Donald R. Meyer, "Learning Motivated by a Manipulation Drive," *Journal of Experimental Psychology* 40, no. 2 (April 1950): 228.

11. Rachel Yehuda et al., "Low Cortisol and Risk for PTSD in Adult Offspring of Holocaust Survivors," *American Journal of Psychiatry* 157, no. 8 (August 2000): 1252–1259.

12. Amy Lehrner and Rachel Yehuda, "Cultural Trauma and Epigenetic Inheritance," *Development and Psychopathology* 30, no. 5 (December 2018): 1763–1777.

13. Bruce H. Lipton, "Maternal Emotions and Human Development," Birth Psychology, available through the Internet Archive, https://web.archive.org/web/20121113215219/https://birthpsychology.com/free-article/maternal-emotions-and-human-development.

14. Mark Wolynn, *It Didn't Start with You: How Inherited Family Trauma Shapes Who We Are and How to End the Cycle* (New York: Penguin, 2017), 25.

15. William C. Shiel, "Definition of Epigenetics," MedicineNet, December 21, 2018, https://www.medicinenet.com/epigenetics/definition.htm.

16. "Scientists Discover How Epigenetic Information Could Be Inherited," Research, University of Cambridge, January 25, 2013, http://www.cam.ac.uk/research/news/scientists-discover-how-epigentic-information-could-be-inherited.

17. Komisar, *Being There*, 36.

18. Diana Divecha, "How Cosleeping Can Help You and Your Baby," *Greater Good Magazine: Science-Based Insights for a Meaningful Life*, February 7, 2020, https://greatergood.berkeley.edu/article/item/how_cosleeping_can_help_you_and_your_baby.

19. James J. McKenna, *Safe Infant Sleep: Expert Answers to Your Cosleeping Questions* (Washington, D.C.: Platypus Media, 2020).

20. Komisar, *Being There*, 101.

21. William Sears, *Nighttime Parenting: How to Get Your Baby and Child to Sleep* (New York: Plume, 1999).

22. James J. McKenna, Helen L. Ball, and Lee T. Gettler, "Mother–Infant Cosleeping, Breastfeeding and Sudden Infant Death Syndrome: What Biological Anthropology Has Discovered About Normal Infant Sleep and Pediatric Sleep Medicine," *American Journal of Phys-*

ical Anthropology: The Official Publication of the American Association of Physical Anthropologists 134, no. S45 (2007): 133–161, 135.

23. Ibid., 147.

24. "Safe Cosleeping Guidelines," University of Notre Dame Mother–Baby Behavioral Sleep Laboratory, accessed December 3, 2020, https://cosleeping.nd.edu/safe-co-sleeping-guidelines.

25. Komisar, *Being There*, 90.

26. Bessel Van der Kolk, *The Body Keeps the Score: Brain, Mind, and Body in the Healing of Trauma* (New York: Penguin, 2015), 217.

Chapter 4

1. Tara Brach, "Healing Addiction: De-Conditioning the Hungry Ghosts," March 29, 2017, https://www.tarabrach.com/healing-addiction.

2. Vincent Iannelli, "Normal Heart Rate for Children," Verywell Family, February 3, 2020, https://www.verywellfamily.com/normal-pulse-rates-for-kids-2634038.

3. "Why Stress Causes People to Overeat," Harvard Mental Health Letter, updated October 13, 2020, https://www.health.harvard.edu/staying-healthy/why-stress-causes-people-to-overeat.

4. Geneen Roth, *When Food Is Love: Exploring the Relationship Between Eating and Intimacy* (New York: Penguin, 1992), 19.

5. Lydia Denworth, "The Loneliness of the 'Social Distancer' Triggers Brain Cravings Akin to Hunger," *Scientific American*, April 2, 2020, https://www.scientificamerican.com/article/the-loneliness-of-the-social-distancer-triggers-brain-cravings-akin-to-hunger.

6. Staci Sprout, e-mail to author, February 19, 2020.

7. Roxane Gay, *Hunger: A Memoir of (My) Body* (New York: Harper, 2018), 166.

8. Ibid., 231.

9. Alexandra Katehakis, *Sexual Addiction as Affect Dysregulation: A Neurobiologically Informed Holistic Treatment* (New York: W. W. Norton, 2016), 57.

10. Roth, *When Food Is Love*, 78.

11. Komisar, *Being There*, 93.

12. Charlotte Davis Kasl, *Women, Sex, and Addiction: A Search for Love and Power* (New York: HarperCollins, 1990), 127.

13. Ibid., 281.

14. Staci Sprout, e-mail to author, February 19, 2020.

Chapter 5

1. David Foster Wallace, "This Is Water," commencement speech at Kenyon College, Gambier, Ohio, May 21, 2005; available at https://fs.blog/2012/04/david-foster-wallace-this-is-water.

2. Anjali Dayal, "We Must Reckon with the Terrible Realities Hidden in Plain Sight," *On Being* blog, April 2, 2018, https://onbeing.org/blog/anjali-dayal-we-must-reckon-with-the-terrible-realities-hidden-in-plain-sight.

3. Evelyn Reed, *Woman's Evolution: From Matriarchal Clan to Patriarchal Family* (New York: Pathfinder Press, 1975), 293.

4. Oscar Serrallach, "Healing the Mother Wound," Goop, accessed December 28, 2020, https://goop.com/wellness/relationships/healing-the-mother-wound.

5. Laura Mulvey, "Visual Pleasure and Narrative Cinema," *Screen* 16, no. 3 (Fall 1975): 6–18.

6. Renee Engeln, *Beauty Sick: How the Cultural Obsession with Appearance Hurts Girls and Women* (New York: Harper Collins, 2017), 45.

7. See Jackson Katz, "Violence Against Women—It's a Men's Issue" (lecture), TEDxFiDiWomen, San Francisco, December 5, 2013; available at https://www.ted.com/talks/jackson_katz_violence_against_women_it_s_a_men_s_issue.

8. Emilie Buchwald, Pamela Fletcher, and Martha Roth, eds., *Transforming a Rape Culture*, rev. ed. (Minneapolis: Milkweed Press, 2005), xi.

9. Katherine Sellgren, "Pornography 'Desensitising Young People,'" BBC News, June 15, 2016, https://www.bbc.com/news/education-36527681.

10. Gail Dines, "The Porn Crisis," accessed November 15, 2020, https://www.gaildines.com/the-porn-crisis.

11. Judith Leavitt, *The Sexual Alarm System: Women's Unwanted Response to Sexual Intimacy and How to Overcome It* (New York: Jason Aronson, 2012), 38.

12. Ibid., 10.

13. See Shelley E. Taylor, "Tend and Befriend Theory," in *Handbook of Theories of Social Psychology,* vol. 1, ed. Paul A. M. Van Lange, Arie W. Kruglanksi, and E. Tori Higgins (Thousand Oaks, CA: Sage, 2012), 32–49.

14. Stanley Schachter, *The Psychology of Affiliation: Experimental Studies of the Sources of Gregariousness* (Redwood City, CA: Stanford University Press, 1959), 71.

15. Shelley E. Taylor et al., "Biobehavioral Responses to Stress in Females: Tend-and-Befriend, Not Fight-or-Flight," *Psychological Review* 107, no. 3 (July 2000): 411–429.

16. Marissa Korbel, "Sometimes You Make Your Rapist Breakfast: Inside the Controversial—and Often Confusing—'Tending Instinct' of Women," *Harper's Bazaar,* April 25, 2018, https://www.harpersbazaar.com/culture/features/a19158567/what-is-rape.

Chapter 6

1. Rachel Yehuda, Sarah L. Halligan, and Robert Grossman, "Childhood Trauma and Risk for PTSD: Relationship to Intergenerational Effects of Trauma, Parental PTSD, and Cortisol Excretion," *Development and Psychopathology* 13, no. 3 (September 2001): 733–753.

2. Meaney, "Maternal Care, Gene Expression, and the Transmission of Individual Differences in Stress Reactivity Across Generations."

3. Heather Schwedel, "*Dirty John* Sneakily Made Its Delicious Mean-Girl Daughters the Real Heroes," *Slate*, January 14, 2019, https://slate.com/culture/2019/01/dirty-john-season-1-finale-review-sisters-daughters.html.

4. Stephanie Nolasco, "'Dirty John' Victim Recalls Daughter Screaming She Had Killed Con Man," *New York Post*, January 11, 2019, https://nypost.com/2019/01/11/dirty-john-victim-recalls-daughter-screaming-she-had-killed-con-man.

5. Stephen W. Porges, *The Polyvagal Theory: Neurophysiological Foundations of Emotions, Attachment, Communication, and Self-Regulation*, Norton Series on Interpersonal Neurobiology (New York: W. W. Norton, 2011).

6. Sarah Peyton, *Your Resonant Self: Guided Meditations and Exercises to Engage Your Brain's Capacity for Healing* (New York: W. W. Norton, 2017), 153.

7. Sara F. Waters, Tessa V. West, and Wendy Berry Mendes, "Stress Contagion: Physiological Covariation Between Mothers and Infants," *Psychological Science* 25, no. 4 (April 2014): 934–942.

8. Gabor Maté, "Love Is Not Enough," produced by KidCare Canada, YouTube video, 4:10, June 1, 2013, https://www.youtube.com/watch?v=Xy57UpKRNEo.

9. "Not All Attention Problems are ADHD," Child Mind Institute, accessed December 3, 2020, https://childmind.org/article/not-all-attention-problems-are-adhd.

10. Centers for Disease Control and Prevention, "About the CDC-Kaiser ACE Study," accessed June 10, 2020, cdc.gov/violenceprevention/acestudy/about.html; Vincent J. Felitti et al., "Relationship of Childhood Abuse and Household Dysfunction to Many of the Leading Causes of Death in Adults: The Adverse Childhood Experiences (ACE) Study," *American Journal of Preventive Medicine* 14, no. 4 (May 1998): 245–258.

11. Simon Partridge, "The Origins of the Adverse Childhood Experiences Movement and Child Sexual Abuse: A Brief History," *Attachment* 13, no. 1 (June 2019): 113–116.

12. Annabelle Timsit, "California's New Surgeon General Changed the Way We Understand Childhood Trauma," Quartz, January 24, 2019, https://qz.com/1530399/nadine-burke-harris-californias-first-surgeon-general-changed-the-way-we-understand-childhood-trauma.

13. Nadine Burke Harris, "How Childhood Trauma Affects Health across a Lifetime," TEDMED, San Francisco, September 2014, https://www.ted.com/talks/nadine_burke_harris_how_childhood_trauma_affects_health_across_a_lifetime.

14. Komisar, *Being There*, 89.

15. Megan R. Gunnar et al., "The Rise in Cortisol in Family Daycare: Associations with Aspects of Care Quality, Child Behavior, and Child Sex," *Child Development* 81, no. 3 (May/June 2010): 851–869.

16. Carolina de Weerth, Jan K. Buitelaar, and Roseriet Beijers, "Infant Cortisol and Behavioral Habituation to Weekly Maternal Separations: Links with Maternal Prenatal cortisol and Psychosocial Stress," *Psychoneuroendocrinology* 38, no. 12 (December 2013): 2863–2874.

17. Komisar, *Being There*, 138.

18. Ibid., 41.

19. Gordon Neufeld, "Preparing for Motherhood: You're More Equipped Than You Think," Tenth Annual Vancouver Neufeld Conference, April 2018, YouTube video, 1:09:23, https://www.youtube.com/watch?v=hz9VWWg1bWY.

20. Komisar, *Being There*, 82.

21. Ibid., 198.

22. Lisa Damour, *Under Pressure: Confronting the Epidemic of Stress and Anxiety in Girls* (New York: Ballantine Books, 2020), xvii.

23. "From Aromatherapy to Anger Management: How Schools are Addressing the 'Crisis' of Childhood Trauma," Child Mind Institute, May 20, 2019, https://childmind.org/news/from-aromatherapy-to-anger-management-how-schools-are-addressing-the-crisis-of-childhood-trauma.

24. Robert M. Post, "Kindling and Sensitization as Models for Affective Episode Recurrence, Cyclicity, and Tolerance Phenomena," *Neuroscience & Biobehavioral Reviews* 31, no. 6 (April 2007): 858–873.

25. Peggy Orenstein, "What Young Women Believe About Their Own Sexual Pleasure," TED talk, October 2016, San Francisco, YouTube video, 17:04, https://www.youtube.com/watch?v=a-BrIRTWnFQ.

26. Peggy Orenstein, "'Girls and Sex' and the Importance of Talking to Young Women About Pleasure," interview by Terry Gross, *Fresh Air*, March 29, 2016, https://www.npr.org/sections/health-shots/2016/03/29/472211301/girls-sex-and-the-importance-of-talking-to-young-women-about-pleasure.

27. Ariel Levy, *Female Chauvinist Pigs: Women and the Rise of Raunch Culture* (New York: Free Press, 2005), 162.

28. Sloane Ryan and Roo Powell, "I'm a 37-Year-Old Mom & I Spent Seven Days Online as an 11-Year-Old Girl. Here's What I Learned," Medium, December 13, 2019, https://medium.com/@sloane_ryan/im-a-37-year-old-mom-i-spent-seven-days-online-as-an-11-year-old-girl-here-s-what-i-learned-9825e81c8e7d.

29. "Social Media Dangers Exposed by Mom Posing as 11-Year-Old," produced by Bark, February 20, 2020, YouTube video, 9:31, https://www.youtube.com/watch?v=dbg4hNHsc_8.

30. Gabor Maté, *In the Realm of Hungry Ghosts: Close Encounters with Addiction* (Berkeley, CA: North Atlantic Books, 2010), 272.

31. Sally Schofield, "The Ins and Outs of Alternate Nostril Breathing," YogaLondon blog, December 18, 2018, https://yogalondon.net/monkey/the-ins-and-outs-of-alternate-nostril-breathing.

Chapter 7

1. Adrienne Brodeur, *Wild Game: My Mother, Her Secret, And Me* (New York: Houghton Mifflin Harcourt, 2019), 14.

2. Ibid., 98.

3. Ibid., 14.

4. Ibid., 98.

5. Teresa D'Astice and William P. Russell, "Enmeshment in Couples and Families," in *Encyclopedia of Couple and Family Therapy*, ed. Jay L. Lebow, Anthony L. Chambers, and Douglas C. Breunlin (New York: Springer International Publishing, 2019), https://doi.org/10.1007/978-3-319-49425-8_1021.

6. Kenneth Adams, *Silently Seduced: When Parents Make Their Children Partners* (Deerfield Beach, FL: Health Communications, Inc., 2011).

7. Patricia A. DeYoung, *Understanding and Treating Chronic Shame: A Relational/Neurobiological Approach* (New York: Routledge, 2015), 95.

8. Brodeur, *Wild Game*, 50.

9. Ibid., 50.

10. Ibid., 97.

11. Korbel, "Sometimes You Make Your Rapist Breakfast."

12. Karin Grossmann et al., "The Uniqueness of the Child–Father Attachment Relationship: Fathers' Sensitive and Challenging Play as a Pivotal Variable in a 16-Year Longitudinal Study," *Social Development* 11, no. 3 (July 2002): 301–337.

13. Lauren Vinopal, "How Fathers of Daughters Can Help Women Make More Money," Ladders, July 22, 2019, https://www.theladders.com/career-advice/how-fathers-of-daughters-can-help-women-make-more-money.

14. Wendy B. Rosen, "On the Integration of Sexuality: Lesbians and Their Mothers," in *Women's Growth in Diversity: More Writings from the Stone Center*, ed. Judith V. Jordan (New York: Guilford Press, 1997), 239–259.

15. Christiane Northrup, *Women's Bodies, Women's Wisdom: Creating Physical and Emotional Health and Healing*, 5th ed. (New York: Bantam, 1994), 4.

Chapter 8

1. George Jessel, quoted in Dial Torgerson, "Judy Garland Dies in London at 47; Tragedy Haunted Star," *Los Angeles Times*, June 23, 1969, https://www.latimes.com/local/obituaries/archives/la-me-judy-garland-19690623-story.html.

2. Caitlin Johnson, "A Film on the French Judy Garland," *CBS Sunday Morning*, June 7, 2007, https://www.cbsnews.com/news/a-film-on-the-french-judy-garland.

3. Judy Garland, *Today Show*, interview by Barbara Walters, May 1967, YouTube video, 19:01, https://www.youtube.com/watch?v=NHJu jYMvY30.

4. Suyin Haynes, "The True Story Behind the Movie *Judy*," *Time*, September 26, 2019, https://time.com/5684673/judy-garland-movie-true-story.

5. Alison Kerr, "The Lasting Love for Edith Piaf, and Her Last Love," *The Herald*, November 20, 2015, https://www.heraldscotland.com/arts_ents/14094390.the-lasting-love-for-edith-piaf-and-her-last-love.

6. Sara Kettler, "Inside Judy Garland's Troubled Youth," updated October 1, 2020, https://www.biography.com/news/judy-garland-facts-bio.

7. "Edith Piath, French Singer," Encyclopedia Britannica, updated December 20, 2020, https://www.britannica.com/biography/Edith-Piaf.

8. Anne Edwards, *Judy Garland: A Biography* (Lanham, MD: Taylor Trade Publishing), 2013.

9. Kerr, "The Lasting Love for Edith Piaf, and Her Last Love," https://www.heraldscotland.com/arts_ents/14094390.the-lasting-love-for-edith-piaf-and-her-last-love.

10. Edwards, *Judy Garland: A Biography*.

11. Megan Romer, "The Tragic Death of French Cabaret Sweetheart Edith Piaf," liveaboutdotcom, June 7, 2018, https://www.liveabout.com/how-did-edith-piaf-die-3552707.

12. Judith Lewis Herman, "Complex PTSD: A Syndrome in Survivors of Prolonged and Repeated Trauma," *Journal of Traumatic Stress* 5, no. 3 (July 1992): 380.

13. Nicole M. Racine et al., "Systematic Review: Predisposing, Precipitating, Perpetuating, and Present Factors Predicting Anticipatory Distress to Painful Medical Procedures in Children," *Journal of Pediatric Psychology* 41, no. 2 (March 2016): 159–181.

14. Susan M. Jay, Mickey Ozolins, Charles H. Elliott, and Steven Caldwell, "Assessment of Children's Distress During Painful Medical Procedures," *Health Psychology* 2, no. 2 (1983): 133.

15. Jennifer Shu, "The American Academy of Pediatrics on Spanking Children: Don't Do It, Ever," interview by Lulu Garcia Navarro, *Weekend Edition*, November 11, 2018, https://www.wbur.org/npr/666646403/the-american-academy-of-pediatrics-on-spanking-children-dont-do-it-ever.

16. Ibid.

17. Julie Brand, *A Mother's Touch: Surviving Mother–Daughter Sexual Abuse* (Bloomington, IN: Trafford, 2007), 153.

18. This list is adapted from "Dynamics of Abuse," National Coalition Against Domestic Violence, accessed January 5, 2021, https://ncadv. org/dynamics-of-abuse.

19. Center on the Developing Child at Harvard University, "In Brief: The Impact of Early Adversity on Children's Development," accessed September 5, 2020, https://developingchild.harvard.edu/ resources/inbrief-the-impact-of-early-adversity-on-childrens-development.

20. "Dynamics of Abuse," National Coalition Against Domestic Violence.

21. Beatrice Beebe and Frank Lachmann, *The Origins of Attachment: Infant Research and Adult Treatment,* Relational Perspectives Book Series (New York: Routledge, 2014).

22. Donald Dutton and Susan L. Painter, "Traumatic Bonding: The Development of Emotional Attachments in Battered Women and Other Relationships of Intermittent Abuse," *Victimology: An International Journal* 6, no. 4 (1981): 139–155.

23. "The Strange Situation–Mary Ainsworth," YouTube video, 3:14, https://www.youtube.com/watch?v=QTsewNrHUHU.

24. Carlo Schuengel et al., "Frightening Maternal Behavior Linking Unresolved Loss and Disorganized Infant Attachment," *Journal of Consulting and Clinical Psychology* 67, no. 1 (March 1999): 54–63, https://doi.org/10.1037/0022-006x.67.1.54.

25. Korbel, "Sometimes You Make Your Rapist Breakfast."

26. Pat Ogden, Kekuni Minton, and Claire Pain, *Trauma and the Body: A Sensorimotor Approach to Psychotherapy,* Norton Series on Interpersonal Neurobiology (New York: W. W. Norton, 2006), 10.

27. Melissa G. Platt and Jennifer J. Freyd, "Betray My Trust, Shame on Me: Shame, Dissociation, Fear, and Betrayal Trauma," *Psychological Trauma: Theory, Research, Practice, and Policy* 7, no. 4 (January 2015): 398–404.

28. Michelle J. Bovin et al., "Tonic Immobility Mediates the Influence of Peritraumatic Fear and Perceived Inescapability on Posttraumatic Stress Symptom Severity Among Sexual Assault Survivors," *Journal of Traumatic Stress: Official Publication of The International Society for Traumatic Stress Studies* 21, no. 4 (August 2008): 402–409.

29. Jennifer Freyd and Pamela Birrell, *Blind to Betrayal: Why We Fool Ourselves We Aren't Being Fooled* (Hoboken, NJ: Wiley & Sons, 2013), 56.

30. Ibid., 95.

31. Van der Kolk, *The Body Keeps the Score*, 133.

32. Stephen W. Porges, "The Polyvagal Theory: New Insights into Adaptive Reactions of the Autonomic Nervous System," *Cleveland Clinic Journal of Medicine* 76, no. 4 (February 2009): S86.

33. Bahar Gholipour, "Strange Case of 'Hyper Empathy' after Brain Surgery," LiveScience, September 11, 2013, https://www.livescience.com/39560-hyper-empathy-case-report.html.

34. Michael Gazzaniga et al., *Cognitive Neuroscience: The Biology of the Mind*, 3rd ed. (New York: W. W. Norton & Company, 2008).

35. DeYoung, *Understanding and Treating Chronic Shame*, 35.

36. See, for example, Ogden, Minton, and Pain, *Trauma and the Body*.

Chapter 9

1. John Bowlby, *A Secure Base: Parent–Child Attachment and Healthy Human Development* (New York: Basic Books, 1990), 140.

2. Peyton, *Your Resonant Self*, 37.

3. Ilanit Hasson-Ohayon et al., "Neuro-cognition and Social Cognition Elements of Social Functioning and Social Quality of Life," *Psychiatry Research* 258 (September 2017): 538–543.

4. Kenneth J. Doka, *Disenfranchised Grief: Recognizing Hidden Sorrow* (Washington, D.C.: Lexington Books, 1989).

5. Elisabeth Kübler-Ross and David Kessler, *On Grief and Grieving: Finding the Meaning of Grief Through the Five Stages of Loss* (New York: Scribner, 2005).

6. Personal communication to the author, January 2019.

7. See Bruce K. Alexander, "Rat Park," accessed January 6, 2021, https://www.brucekalexander.com/articles-speeches/rat-park.

8. Asheville Emporium, "Wonder Woman 78 Years Strong," http://asheville-emporium.com/wonder-woman-78-years-strong.

9. DeYoung, *Understanding and Treating Chronic Shame*, 162.

10. Ibid., 87.

Chapter 10

1. Susan Forward, *Mothers Who Can't Love: A Healing Guide for Daughters* (New York: Harper Collins, 2013), 13.

2. Kenneth J. Gruber, Susan H. Cupio, and Christina F. Dobson, "Impact of Doulas on Healthy Birth Outcomes," *Journal of Perinatal Education* 22, no. 1 (Winter 2013): 49–58.

3. "Meet Darcia," Evolved Nest, accessed January 8, 2021, https://evolvednest.org/about.

Conclusion

1. "Governor Newsom Announces $42 Million to Protect Foster Youth and Families Impacted by COVID-19," Office of Governor Gavin Newsom, April 13, 2020, https://www.gov.ca.gov/2020/04/13/governor-newsom-announces-42-million-to-protect-foster-youth-and-families-impacted-by-covid-19.

2. Danielle Roubinov, Nicole R. Bush, and Thomas W. Boyce, "How a Pandemic Could Advance the Science of Early Adversity," *JAMA Pediatrics* 174, no. 12 (July 2020): 1131–1132.

3. "The Medical Value of Hugs," CBS News, August 2, 2020, https://www.cbsnews.com/news/the-medical-value-of-hugs.

4. Jim Alexrod, "The Smile Behind the Mask," CBS News, September 6, 2020, https://www.cbsnews.com/news/the-smile-behind-the-mask.

5. Denworth, "The Loneliness of the 'Social Distancer' Triggers Brain Cravings Akin to Hunger," https://www.scientificamerican.com/article/the-loneliness-of-the-social-distancer-triggers-brain-cravings-akin-to-hunger.

6. Margaret Renkl, *Late Migrations: A Natural History of Love and Loss* (Minneapolis: Milkweed, 2019), 218.

ACKNOWLEDGMENTS

Hay House team, thank you for selecting my book for publication. Your support means *Mother Hunger: How Adult Daughters Can Understand and Heal from Lost Nurturance, Protection, and Guidance* will find the women who need it.

Guidance is essential for every writer who wants to share a published manuscript with the world. Thank you to Ami McConnell, author and professional editor, for masterfully digesting the concepts and overall mission for this book. Your expertise guided these pages home. Kacie Main, thank you for reworking the first chapter with beautiful insight. Corrine Casanova, thank you for checking my research and cheering me on. KN Literary team, thank you for helping me with my book proposal. Thank you Mary O'Donohue for getting me "media ready." Jenn at Mixtusmedia, thank you for the social media guidance.

Protection is essential for writing. Just as the world needed safe refuge from a sinister pandemic, our home caught fire. We needed protection. We gathered our kittens and essentials, and fled to my parents' home a few hours away. Their protection allowed me to continue writing.

An author needs nurturance. I'm forever grateful to the special people who nurtured me while I spent hours at my desk. Melinda, my bonus mother and friend, affirmed this project every chance she could. Virtual assistant Audrey Isbell reminded to write this book even when I didn't want to. Dear friend Jennifer Acker sent loving texts each morning, sharing an emotional refuge. Margaret Renkl and Millie, writer, neighbor, and special pup, offered writing empathy when our daily walks intersected. Julieann Myers felt the essence of this book and reflected it back to me. Robin

Satyshur always made time for me to talk through a chapter. Britt Frank fueled me for social media and dentist appointments. Michelle Mays opened her home, traveled to mine, shared edits and tireless feedback, and reminded me of the need for this book.

Living with a therapist/writer during a global pandemic is some kind of cruel joke. In spite of adversity, Chris McDaniel kept the firewood stocked, the snack cabinet full, and managed writing mood swings with grace. Chris, thank you for the emotional space to write and the tireless hours discussing Mother Hunger. Garrett, thank you for the regular check-ins. Your life is magnificent to behold. I'm grateful to be your mother.

ABOUT THE AUTHOR

Kelly McDaniel, LPC, NCC, CSAT is a licensed professional counselor and author who specializes in treating women who experience addictive relational patterns. A pioneer in her field, McDaniel is the first clinician to name Mother Hunger as an attachment injury and explore the repercussions of bonding to an emotionally compromised mother. Kelly teaches workshops and speaks to audiences nationwide about Mother Hunger. *Ready to Heal* is her first book. Website: kellymcdanieltherapy.com

Hay House Titles of Related Interest

We hope you enjoyed this Hay House book. If you'd like to receive our online catalog featuring additional information on Hay House books and products, or if you'd like to find out more about the Hay Foundation, please contact:

Hay House, Inc., P.O. Box 5100, Carlsbad, CA 92018-5100
(760) 431-7695 or (800) 654-5126
(760) 431-6948 (fax) or (800) 650-5115 (fax)
www.hayhouse.com® • www.hayfoundation.org

———

Published in Australia by: Hay House Australia Pty. Ltd.,
18/36 Ralph St., Alexandria NSW 2015
Phone: 612-9669-4299 • *Fax:* 612-9669-4144
www.hayhouse.com.au

Published in the United Kingdom by: Hay House UK, Ltd.,
The Sixth Floor, Watson House, 54 Baker Street, London W1U 7BU
Phone: +44 (0)20 3927 7290 • *Fax:* +44 (0)20 3927 7291
www.hayhouse.co.uk

Published in India by: Hay House Publishers India,
Muskaan Complex, Plot No. 3, B-2, Vasant Kunj, New Delhi 110 070
Phone: 91-11-4176-1620 • *Fax:* 91-11-4176-1630
www.hayhouse.co.in

———

Access New Knowledge.
Anytime. Anywhere.

Learn and evolve at your own pace
with the world's leading experts.

www.hayhouseU.com